Key Comprehension Book 3

CONTENTS

UNIT 1

The disappearing days

"Oh dear!" groaned the King of Incrediblania. "Monday again, washing day; the house full of soapy smells and the grounds full of washing. I positively dislike Mondays, and I can't stand washing day!"

"Why not abolish it, Your Majesty?" suggested the Lord Chancellor, who didn't like Monday either, because that was the day he had to put on his heavy wig and elaborate robes and sign no end of documents.

"Hm," said the King. He looked up "abolish" in the royal dictionary and found it meant to do away with something and stop having it. "An excellent idea!" he cried. "Yes, indeed, we shall abolish Mondays, and with them this horrible, damp, smelly, uncomfortable washing day business."

He sent for the Astronomer Royal and said, "It is our royal wish that there shall be no more Mondays in the kingdom of Incrediblania. Kindly abolish them, will you?"

"Ah, now, Majesty," said the Astronomer Royal. "And what does your Majesty, in his wisdom, wish to do with the days that used to be Mondays?"

"Oh!" said the King, who hadn't even thought of that. "That makes it sort of awkward, doesn't it?"

"It doesn't do anything of the kind," said the Queen, who had just come in from seeing that the royal washing was pegged out with becoming royal dignity. "All you have to do is have two Sundays and then go straight on to Tuesday, so the day that was Monday becomes a second Sunday." She sat down on the throne feeling delighted because she liked Sundays as she had her breakfast in bed then.

"Yes, of course," said the King, trying to look as if he had thought of it himself. "Two Sundays, then go straight on to Tuesday."

Norman Hunter from *The Frantic Phantom* (Puffin Books)

1   Why did the King of Incrediblania hate washing days? *(2 marks)*

     a) He found washing days very tiring and he didn't like ironing.

     b) He found it difficult to get anything done because everyone was so cross.

     c) He didn't like the smell and having the palace gardens full of washing.

2   Why did the Lord Chancellor hate Mondays? *(2 marks)*

     a) He didn't like the smell of soap.

     b) He had to sign lots of papers on Mondays and wear his official costume.

     c) He only pretended that he hated Mondays.

3   What does "abolish" mean? *(2 marks)*

     a) It means to announce something.

     b) It means to stop something by law.

     c) It means to disagree with something.

4   Which four adjectives did the King use to describe washing days? *(4 marks)*

     a) wet, steamy, smelly, uncomfortable

     b) horrible, soapy, tiring, hot

     c) uncomfortable, smelly, damp, horrible

5   What did the Queen do on washing days? *(2 marks)*

     a) She made sure the washing was hung on the line properly.

     b) She made sure the water was hot enough to wash the clothes properly.

     c) She had breakfast in bed.

6   How did the Queen feel about abolishing Mondays? *(2 marks)*

     a) She liked the idea.

     b) She didn't really like the idea.

     c) She thought it was a silly idea.

7   Which statement about the King is true? *(1 mark)*

     a) He has a special dictionary.

     b) He has a very long beard.

     c) He is a very clever man.

UNIT 2

A thoroughly modern Grandmama

I've become a world authority
on how grandmothers *ought* to look
because dotty dear old ladies
smile from every picture book.

They're usually round and cuddly
with grey hair and a hat.
They drink endless cups of milky tea,
always, always have a cat.

They are very good at knitting
and they'll mind you for the day –
I'm sure picture book grannies are
all very well, but boring in their way.

Now *my* grandmother hasn't read
the books – she hasn't got a clue
about the way she should behave
and the things she mustn't do.

She's always on a diet
and I'm sure she dyes her hair,
and I haven't got a grandpapa so
her boyfriend's sometimes there.

She wears jazzy shirts and skin-tight
jeans, jangles bracelets on her arm.
She zooms me around in her little car,
strapped-in, and safe from harm.

She's a busy lady with a job
and a diary to book me in.
She doesn't knit and doesn't drink tea,
preferring coffee, wine or gin!

My grandmother's a complete disaster
as ordinary grannies go –
but I wouldn't want to swap her
or I'd have done it long ago!

Moira Andrew from *All in the Family* ed. John Foster (Oxford University Press)

1   Picture book grandmothers are usually round and cuddly.
     How do we know from the poem that this grandmother was
     probably quite slim? *(1.5 marks)*
     We know that she was probably quite slim because the poem says...

2   Picture book grandmothers have grey hair. How do we know from the
     poem that this grandmother didn't have grey hair? *(1.5 marks)*
     We know that she didn't have grey hair because the poem says...

3   Picture book grandmothers are very good at knitting. Did this
     grandmother knit? *(1.5 marks)*
     We know that she...

4   What kind of clothes did this grandmother like to wear? *(1.5 marks)*
     She liked to wear...

5   How do we know that the girl liked her grandmother being different
     from picture book grandmothers? *(1.5 marks)*
     We know because she says she wouldn't...

6   What does "zooms" (verse 6) tell you about the way this grandmother drove?
     (1.5 marks)
     "Zooms" tells me that she drove...

7   Why did the girl's grandmother have to use a diary to arrange their meetings?
     (1.5 marks)
     She had to use a diary because...

8   The girl describes her grandmother as "a complete disaster / as ordinary
     grannies go". What does she mean by this? *(1.5 marks)*
     The girl means that...

9   Which word rhymes with "do" in verse 4? *(1.5 marks)*
     The word that rhymes with "do" is...

10   Which word rhymes with "there" in verse 5? *(1.5 marks)*
     The word that rhymes with "there" is...

UNIT 3

Insects, colour and camouflage

Insects use colour to send a variety of messages or to conceal themselves from predators.

Warning colours in nature

Combinations of red and black or yellow and black are used as warning colours. They warn birds that insects, such as ladybirds, taste terrible. Similarly, the colours warn that bees and wasps can inflict painful stings.

Flash colours

Some grasshoppers use both colour and camouflage to great effect. At rest, their brown and green colours camouflage them among plants and twigs. If they are disturbed by a bird, they fly off, flashing brightly-coloured hind wings. Then, quite suddenly, they land again and disappear into the background. The confused bird is left searching for its prey.

Mimics

Quite harmless insects, such as clearwing moths, hover flies, bee flies and some beetles mimic the warning colours of wasps, bees and ladybirds. Predators are usually fooled and leave them alone.

Eyespots

Some butterflies, moths and their caterpillars have large, staring eye-like markings which are flashed to scare off birds. The birds are thought to mistake the eyes for those of one of their own enemies, for example, a cat.

Frightening face

The green and brown colouring of the puss moth caterpillar camouflages it among willow and poplar leaves. But if something disturbs it, it rears up, flashing false eyes and lashing out with its tentacle-like hind legs. If this doesn't work, it squirts formic acid at its attacker.

Camouflage

Many insects camouflage themselves by looking like something else, for example, twigs, thorns, leaves or flowers. With their long, slender bodies, stick insects can hold themselves still and look exactly like the twigs they are resting on. They will even sway as if they are twigs being blown by a breeze. Their eggs, too, are camouflaged to look like plant seeds. ⇨

▲ *The Io moth has markings which look like eyes.*

◄ *The yellow and black colouring of the hover fly warns birds not to eat it.*

▼ *The Eumorpha typhon moth is camouflaged amongst the dead leaves and twigs.*

Industrial colouring

Peppered moths in Britain and Europe have evolved two forms of camouflage to suit their particular environments. In country areas, they are light and speckled to hide them against lichen-covered tree trunks. But in industrialised areas, they have evolved a darker colouring to match soot-blackened tree trunks.

Other insects have also undergone this process, which is called industrial melanism. There are darker forms of many moths and grasshoppers.

▲ *The peppered moth*

Anita Garner from *Nature Detectives: Insects* (Franklin Watts)

Answer in sentences.

1   What colour combinations tell birds that an insect would taste terrible if they ate it? (*1 mark*)

2   Explain how some butterflies can scare birds away just by using their wings. (*2 marks*)

3   Why is it very difficult to see grasshoppers when they are among plants and twigs? (*1 mark*)

4   Why are stick insects very hard to see when they are on twigs? (*2 marks*)

5   What do the eggs of stick insects look like? (*1 mark*)

6   Is it true that grasshoppers can fly? (*1 mark*)

7   Is it true that birds eat caterpillars? (*1 mark*)

8   Read the "Flash colours" section again. Which word in the section means "bewildered"? (*2 marks*)

9   Explain what "camouflage" means. (*2 marks*)

10   Explain what "slender" means. (*2 marks*)

The air raid

This story takes place during the Second World War. Harry's house has just been hit by a bomb.

Harry got up slowly. He hurt nearly all over, but not so badly that he couldn't move. The man gave him a hand and pulled him up out of the shelter. Harry peered up the garden. He could see quite well because the sky to the west was glowing pink.

There was no greenhouse left.

There was no house left. The houses to each side were still standing, though their windows had gone, and their slates were off.

"Where's our house?"

There was a silence. Then the man with the moustache said, "What's yer name, son?" Harry told him.

"And what was yer Dad's name? And yer Mam's?" He wrote it all down in a notebook, like the police did, when they caught you scrumping apples. He gave them Dulcie's name, too. He tried to be helpful. Then he said, "Where *are* they?" and began to run up the garden path.

The man grabbed him, quick and rough.

"You can't go up there, son. There's a gas leak. A bad gas leak. Pipe's fractured. It's dangerous. It's against the law to go up there."

"But my Mam and Dad're up there..."

"Nobody's up there now, son. Come down to the Rest Centre. They'll tell you all about it at the Rest Centre." ⇨

9

Harry just let himself be led off across some more gardens. It was easy, because all the fences were blown flat. They went up the path of Number Five. The white faces of the Humphreys, who lived at Number Five, peered palely from the door of their shelter. They let him pass, without saying anything to him.

In the road, the wardens who were leading him met two other wardens.

"Any luck at Number Nine?"

"Just this lad..."

There was a long, long silence. Then one of the other wardens said, "We found the family from Number Seven. They were in the garden. The bomb caught them as they were running for the shelter..."

"They all right?"

"Broken arms and legs, I think. But they'll live. Got them away in the ambulance."

Harry frowned. The Simpsons lived at Number Seven. There was some fact he should be able to remember about the Simpsons. But he couldn't. It was all... mixed up.

Robert Westall from *The Kingdom by the Sea* (Egmont Books)

 Choose the correct answer to each question and write it out.
(1.5 marks for each correct answer)

1   Where was Harry when the bomb fell?
a) Harry was in his bedroom.
b) Harry was in the shelter in the house.
c) Harry was in the shelter in the garden.

2   Why did the warden want to know the names of Harry's mother and father?
a) He wanted the names for official records.
b) He wanted to contact them to let them know where Harry was.
c) He wanted to tell them that Harry had been scrumping apples.

3   Why didn't the warden answer when Harry said, "Where's our house"?
a) He didn't know where Harry lived.
b) He didn't know where Harry's house had gone.
c) He didn't want to tell Harry that his house had been blown up by a bomb.

4   If a gas pipe is "fractured", what has happened to it?

    a) It has gone rusty.

    b) It has got blocked.

    c) It has been broken.

5   Why did Harry run up the garden path?

    a) He wanted to find his parents.

    b) He wanted to get something to eat.

    c) He wanted to find his model.

6   What was the number of Harry's house?

    a) His house was number 5.

    b) His house was number 7.

    c) His house was number 9.

7   Why did the warden want to get Harry to the Rest Centre as quickly as possible?

    a) He knew Harry's parents would be there.

    b) He wanted to get Harry away from the bomb site and thought Harry would need help and support after what had happened.

    c) He thought the exercise would be good for Harry.

8   Why were the Humphrey family so pale?

    a) They were in a state of shock.

    b) They had been ill.

    c) They never got any fresh air.

9   Where were the Simpson family when the bomb fell?

    a) They were in the ambulance.

    b) They were running to the Rest Centre.

    c) They were in their garden.

10   Which sentence best describes Harry's feelings at the end of the passage?

    a) He felt angry and disappointed.

    b) He felt frightened and unhappy.

    c) He had a bad stomach ache.

UNIT 5

Remember me?

Remember me?
I am the boy who sought friendship;
The boy you turned away.
I the boy who asked you
If I too might play.

I the face at the window
When your party was inside,
I the lonely figure
That walked away and cried.

I the one who hung around,
A punchbag for your games.
Someone you could kick and beat,
Someone to call names.

But how strange is the change
After time has hurried by.
Four years have passed since then
Now I'm not so quick to cry.

I'm bigger and I'm stronger,
I've grown a foot in height,
Suddenly I'm popular
And YOU'RE left out the light.

I could, if I wanted,
Be so unkind to you.
I would only have to say
And the other boys would do.

But the memory of my pain
Holds back the revenge I'd
planned
And instead, I feel much
stronger
By offering you my hand.

Ray Mather from *New Caribbean Junior Readers*
(Ginn & Company)

1 To whom was the boy speaking when he said, "Remember me"? *(1 mark)*

2 List all the ways in which the boy had been made to feel hurt and rejected four years before. *(2.5 marks)*

3 In what ways is he different now? *(1.5 marks)*

4 Why did the boy not take his revenge when he had the chance? *(2 marks)*

5 What did he do instead of taking revenge? *(2 marks)*

6 Why did he "feel much stronger" when he decided not to take revenge? *(2 marks)*

7 What does "sought" (line 2) mean? *(1 mark)*

8 What does "too" (line 5) mean? *(1 mark)*

9 What does "punchbag" (line 11) mean? *(1 mark)*

10 What does "popular" (line 20) mean? *(1 mark)*

UNIT 6

Earthquakes

Once every 30 seconds somewhere in the world the Earth shakes slightly. These earth tremors are strong enough to be felt, but cause no damage. However, every few months a major earthquake occurs. The land shakes so violently that roads break up, forming huge cracks, and buildings and bridges collapse, causing many deaths. Earthquakes are caused by the movements of huge plates of rock in the Earth's crust. They occur in places that lie on the boundaries where these plates meet, such as the San Andreas fault which runs 435 km (270 miles) through central California.

Earthquakes

There are two different scales for measuring earthquakes: the Richter scale and the Modified Mercalli scale.

Richter Scale

The Richter scale measures the strength of an earthquake at its source and takes account of the distance from the earthquake. The scale below gives an indication of the probable effects of earthquakes of particular magnitudes.

RICHTER SCALE	
Magnitude	**Probable effects**
1	Detectable only by instruments.
2–3	Can just be felt by people.
4–5	May cause slight damage.
6	Fairly destructive.
7	A major earthquake.
8–9	A very destructive earthquake.

Modified Mercalli Scale

The Modified Mercalli scale measures how much an earthquake shakes the ground at a particular place. This is called the felt intensity and the scale gives a list of descriptions of earthquake effects.

MODIFIED MERCALLI SCALE

Intensity	Probable effects
1	Not felt by people.
2	May be felt by some people on upper floors.
3	Detected indoors. Hanging objects may swing.
4	Hanging objects swing. Doors and windows rattle.
5	Felt outdoors by most people. Small objects moved or upset.
6	Felt by everyone. Furniture moves. Trees and bushes shake.
7	Difficult for people to stand. Buildings damaged, loose bricks fall.
8	Major damage to buildings. Branches of trees break.
9	General panic. Large cracks in ground. Some buildings collapse.
10	Large landslides occur. Many buildings are destroyed.
11	Major ground disturbances. Railway lines buckle.
12	Damage is nearly total. Large objects thrown into the air.

from *The Dorling Kindersley Illustrated Encyclopedia*

 Write out the sentences that are true. *(15 marks)*

1 California is a high-risk area for earthquakes.

2 Every 30 seconds there is a major earthquake somewhere in the world.

3 Earthquakes are caused by huge plates of rock moving in the Earth's crust.

4 A major earthquake takes place every few months.

5 The Richter scale measures the noise made by earthquakes.

6 Scientists always know when an earthquake is going to happen.

7 A major earthquake registers 7 on the Richter scale.

8 During major earthquakes, buildings are destroyed.

9 The Richter scale is hardly ever used now.

10 The Modified Mercalli scale measures how much the ground shakes.

The runt

"Where's Papa going with that axe?" said Fern to her mother as they were setting the table for breakfast.

"Out to the hoghouse," replied Mrs Arable. "Some pigs were born last night."

"I don't see why he needs an axe," continued Fern, who was only eight.

"Well," said her mother, "one of the pigs is a runt. It's very small and weak, and it will never amount to anything. So your father has decided to do away with it."

"Do *away* with it?" shrieked Fern. "You mean *kill* it? Just because it's smaller than the others?"

Mrs Arable put a pitcher of cream on the table. "Don't yell, Fern!" she said. "Your father is right. The pig would probably die anyway."

Fern pushed a chair out of the way, and ran outdoors. The grass was wet and the earth smelled of springtime. Fern's sneakers were sopping by the time she caught up with her father.

"Please don't kill it!" she sobbed. "It's unfair."

Mr Arable stopped walking.

"Fern," he said gently, "you will have to learn to control yourself."

"Control myself?" yelled Fern. "This is a matter of life and death, and you talk about *controlling* myself." Tears ran down her cheeks and she took hold of the axe and tried to pull it out of her father's hand.

"Fern," said Mr Arable, "I know more about raising a litter of pigs than you do. A weakling makes trouble. Now run along!"

"But it's unfair," cried Fern. "The pig couldn't help being born small, could it? If *I* had been very small at birth, would you have killed *me*?"

Mr Arable smiled. "Certainly not," he said, looking down at his daughter with love. "But this is different. A little girl is one thing, a little runty pig is another."

"I see no difference," replied Fern, still hanging on to the axe. "This is the most terrible case of injustice I ever heard of."

A queer look came over John Arable's face. He seemed almost ready to cry himself.

"All right," he said. "You can go back to the house and I will bring the runt when I come in. I'll let you raise it on a bottle, like a baby. Then you'll see what trouble a pig can be."

When Mr Arable returned to the house half an hour later, he carried a carton under his arm. Fern was upstairs changing her sneakers. The kitchen table was set for breakfast, and the room smelt of coffee, bacon, damp plaster, and wood-smoke from the stove.

"Put it on her chair!" said Mrs Arable. Mr Arable set the carton down at Fern's place. Then he walked to the sink and washed his hands and dried them on the roller towel.

Fern came slowly down the stairs. Her eyes were red from crying. As she approached her chair, the carton wobbled, and there was a scratching noise. Fern looked at her father. Then she lifted the lid of the carton. There, inside, looking up at her, was the newborn pig.

E.B. White from *Charlotte's Web* (Puffin Books)

Answer in sentences.

1   What was Fern's surname? *(1 mark)*

2   How old was Fern? *(1 mark)*

3   What was Mr Arable going to do with the axe? *(2 marks)*

4   What did he decide to give Fern to look after? *(1 mark)*

5   What do you find out about what Mr Arable's personality is like from this passage? Include all the details you can find. *(4 marks)*

6   What do the following words mean? *(1 mark each)*
    a) **hoghouse**
    b) **sneakers**
    c) **pitcher**

7   Which word in the passage means "the smallest, weakest pig in the litter"? *(1 mark)*

8   What did the kitchen smell of at breakfast time? *(2 marks)*

A Martian comes to stay

It was on the second day of Peter's holiday with his grandmother that the Martian came to the cottage. There was a knock at the door and when he went to open it there was this small green person with webbed feet and eyes on the end of stumpy antennae who said, perfectly politely, "I wonder if I might bother you for the loan of a spanner?"

"Sure," said Peter. "I'll ask my gran."

Gran was in the back garden, it being a nice sunny day. Peter said, "There's a Martian at the door who'd like to borrow a spanner."

Gran looked at him over her knitting. "Is there, dear? Have a look in grandad's toolbox, there should be one there."

That's not what your grandmother would have said? No, nor mine either, but Peter's gran was an unusual lady, as you will discover. Grandad had died a few years earlier and she lived alone in this isolated cottage in the country, growing vegetables and keeping chickens, and Peter liked going to stay with her more than almost anything he could think of. Gran was not like most people. She was unflappable and what you might call open-minded, which accounts for everything that happened next.

Peter found the spanner and took it back to the Martian, who held out a rather oddly constructed hand and thanked him warmly.

"We've got some trouble with the gears or something and had to make an emergency landing. And now the mechanic says he left his tools back at base. I ask you! It's all a mystery to me – I'm just the steward. Anyway – thanks a lot. I'll bring it back in a minute." And he padded away up the lane. There was no one around, but then there wasn't likely to be: the cottage was a quarter of a mile from the village and hardly anyone came by except the occasional farm tractor and the odd holiday maker who'd got lost. Peter went back into the garden.

"Should have offered him a cup of tea," said Gran. "He'll have had a fair journey, I shouldn't wonder."

"Yes," said Peter. "I didn't think of that."

In precisely three minutes' time there was a knock at the door.
The Martian was there, looking distinctly agitated. He said, "They've gone."

"Who's gone?" said Peter.

"The others. The spaceship. All of them. They've taken off and left me."

Penelope Lively from *A Sackful of Stories for Eight-year olds* ed. P. Thomson (Corgi Books)

 Answer in sentences. *(1.5 marks each)*

1 How did Peter react when he opened the door and found a Martian there?

2 What was Gran doing when the Martian knocked at the door?

3 What is an emergency landing?

4 Why didn't the Martians have their own toolbox in the spaceship?

5 The Martian "padded away up the lane." What does "padded" mean?

6 Why was Gran's reaction so unusual when Peter told her there was a Martian at the door?

7 Gran's cottage was isolated. What does "isolated" mean?

8 Why did Gran wish that she had offered the Martian a cup of tea?

9 Gran's husband was dead. Which of the following words means a woman whose husband is dead?

orphan   widow   widower

10 Why was the Martian agitated when he came back?

U N I T
9

Ladislao Biro

You may never have heard of Ladislao Biro, but you have certainly heard of the pen he invented – the ballpoint pen, or biro. Before Biro invented his pen, people wrote with fountain pens. The ink smudged and blotted and the pens sometimes leaked. In the 1930s Biro was a magazine editor in Budapest in Hungary. He noticed that the inks which the magazine's printers used dried very quickly. Biro wondered if quick-drying inks could be used in pens. He came up with the idea of a tube of ink with a free-moving ball on the end. As a person wrote, the ball collected ink from the tube and rolled it on to the paper. The pen would be cheap and could be thrown away when the ink ran out.

Biro began to work on his invention but before he could patent it the Second World War broke out. Biro left war-torn Europe and fled to Buenos Aires in Argentina. There, he and his brother Georg, who was a chemist, began to improve the pen. In the early 1940s Biro began to manufacture his new pen, the biro.

Biro did not have enough money to start a big manufacturing company. In 1944, he sold his invention to another company, who began to mass-produce the pen for the British and American armed forces. The servicemen and women liked the pens because they did not leak and were easy to carry around.

Biro was pleased that his pen was popular, but he did not gain much from his invention. The biro was later sold to the French firm, Bic, who now sell twelve million pens a day. Biro sank into obscurity in South America. His name, however, has become a household word.

1900	*born in Hungary*
1938	*applies for patent for first ballpoint pen*
1939	*flees from Hungary to escape Nazis; goes to France, Spain and then Argentina*
c. 1943	*begins to manufacture pens*
1944	*sells invention*

Jacqueline Dineen from *Twenty Inventors* (Wayland Publishers Ltd)

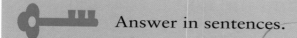 Answer in sentences.

1 Where was Ladislao Biro born? *(1 mark)*

2 How did working as a magazine editor help him to invent the biro? *(1 mark)*

3 Why did he sell his invention in 1944? *(2 marks)*

4 Which French firm still manufactures his invention? *(2 marks)*

5 Find four reasons in the passage for the popularity of ballpoint pens. *(2 marks)*

6 Is it true that Ladislao Biro made a huge fortune out of his invention? *(1 mark)*

7 In what year did Ladislao Biro leave Hungary? *(1 mark)*

8 What happened to Biro's invention in 1943? *(1 mark)*

9 "Biro sank into obscurity in South America." Explain in your own words what this means. *(2 marks)*

10 "His name has become a household word." Explain in your own words what this means. *(2 marks)*

The woman, the boy and the lion

This is an African folk-tale with a moral:
making friends sometimes needs time and patience.

Once, long ago in Ethiopia, there lived a woman named Fanaye who
was a widow. After a while she married a good sort of man whose
wife had died, leaving him with one little boy. So now the little boy
had a stepmother. I don't know why it was – perhaps he had heard
tales about bad stepmothers – but anyhow this little boy would hardly
speak to Fanaye, just turned his head away if he saw she was looking
at him and never said good night or good morning or let her kiss him.

Now this Fanaye was a nice woman. She had no children of her
own and she had thought how nice it would be to have this little boy
to look after.

But no! Do what she would, however hard she tried she couldn't
get the little boy to be friends with her, not even if she cooked specially
nice food for him or tried to cuddle him and tell him stories.

Poor Fanaye asked all her friends what she ought to do, but
none of them could suggest anything new, just all the things she
had tried already.

Her husband often had to go away on long journeys and she
was afraid that he would begin to think she had been unkind to
his little son.

At last she went to the Wise Man.

"What am I to do!" she said. "My little stepson doesn't love me!"
and she told the Wise Man all about the things she had tried, and how
the little boy didn't eat his food, and how, if she tried to pick him up
and kiss him, the child only struggled away and burst into tears.

"Help me, if you can, O Wise Man. My husband is sure to believe I
am being unkind to his little son."

"I think I can help you," said the Wise Man, after thinking. "But I
shall most likely need to make a very strong spell. Now for the spell
you will have to bring me some hairs from the tail of the black-maned
lion. Mind! You must get the hairs yourself, otherwise the spell won't
work. Bring them as soon as you can."

Poor Fanaye didn't know what to do. None of the tame lions were the black-maned kind! She herself wasn't very big or very brave and she was dreadfully afraid of the wild lions and always ran as fast as she could past a certain lion's cave on the side of the mountain to get water from the spring. Now and then she could hear the lion roaring inside the cave and every night they were careful to shut up their cow and calf safely in the shed for fear this lion should kill them. The dangerous time was when he came out of his cave and prowled about at dusk.

So when the Wise Man said that, the poor woman wondered how she could ever come near a lion, still less get hairs from his tail? So she went home very down-hearted. But that evening it was just the same with the little boy. He wouldn't speak to her, he turned his head away if she looked at him, wouldn't eat the supper she had cooked for him and crept away to bed without a word.

Well, that was dreadful. So at last she said to herself, "I will try to do it!"

But how? All that night she thought and thought and at last she decided on a plan. Next evening she took some meat with her when she went (rather late) to get water and, on her way home again, she left the meat at the mouth of the lion's cave, but she was too frightened to wait and see what would happen. ⟹

Next evening she did the same thing but this time she didn't run away but hid behind a tree to watch. Sure enough, after a while, the lion came out, saw the meat, sniffed at it and then lay down comfortably to eat it holding the meat between the paws. She saw that he was a big black-maned lion. He moved his tail about as he ate and the hairs at the end of his tail were black too.

"Oh dear," she thought, "the Wise Man would have known if I'd tried cheating and gone to the town and got one of the keepers to give me hairs off the tail of one of the Emperor's tame lions."

She thought this black-maned wild lion was a beautiful beast but she was very much afraid of him.

Next day – that was the third day – she brought meat again and this time, the third time, she stood waiting, still a good way off, but where the lion could see her.

On the fourth evening she sat down much nearer, and on the fifth evening she held out the meat to him in her hand – but she had to drop it at the last minute.

So it went on, till after a while there came a day when the lion was taking meat from her quite peaceably.

At last (very carefully, so as not to pull), she was able to snip, each day, a few of the beautiful hairs from the end of his tail while he contentedly crunched meat and bone. When she had got a nice little bunch, Fanaye – very well pleased – went off to the Wise Man again.

"Here is the hair from the lion's tail that you asked for," she said to him, holding it out. "What must I do now?"

"Well done, Fanaye," said the Wise Man. "It must have been quite difficult! How did you manage it?"

So then Fanaye told the Wise Man all about it – how she had brought meat and put it outside the lion's cave but how at first she had been too frightened even to see if he would eat it and how she had run away. Then how, day by day, she had gone on bringing meat and had come a little nearer and how, soon, he would take the meat quite peaceably from her hand and how, in the end, he had allowed her to cut, each day, a tail hair or two and how careful she had to be not to pull.

"That was very well done!" said the Wise Man. "You were very careful, you didn't startle him and so in the end he trusted you. The spell you asked for? You know it now. Make friends slowly; don't startle him. Surely it will be easier with a human child than a wild, black-maned lion?"

And so it was. Fanaye was very patient, but at last the little boy got quite friendly, ate his food nicely and used to sit on her lap while she told him stories.

And the story he liked best was one about a wild, black-maned lion.

from *New Caribbean Junior Reader 5* (Ginn & Company)

 Answer in sentences.

1   What did Fanaye do to try to make the little boy like her? *(2 marks)*

2   Why do you think the little boy was so unfriendly at first? *(2 marks)*

3   This story has a moral (that making friends sometimes needs time and patience). What is another word for "moral"? *(1 mark)*

4   Why did the wise man make Fanaye bring him the hair from the lion's tail when he could have told her right away that she would just have to be very patient? *(1 mark)*

5   In what ways was the boy like the wild black-maned lion? *(1 mark)*

6   What do you find out about what Fanaye's personality is like from this story? Include all the details you can find. *(2 marks)*

7   Find the following words in the passage. What other words could be used instead without changing the meaning? *(1 mark each)*

a) tales (paragraph 1)

b) down-hearted (paragraph 11)

c) peaceably (8 paragraphs from the end)

d) contentedly (7 paragraphs from the end)

e) manage (5 paragraphs from the end)

f) trusted (3 paragraphs from the end)

Tom

The striking of the grandfather clock became a familiar sound to Tom, especially in the silence of those nights when everyone else was asleep. He did not sleep. He would go to bed at the usual time, and then lie awake or half-awake for hour after hour. He had never suffered from sleeplessness before in his life, and wondered at it now; but a certain tightness and unease in his stomach should have given him an answer. Sometimes he would doze, and then in his half-dreaming, he became two persons, and one of him would not go to sleep but selfishly insisted on keeping the other awake with a little muttering monologue on whipped cream and shrimp sauce and rum butter and real mayonnaise and all the other rich variety of his diet nowadays. From that Tom was positively relieved to wake up again.

Aunt Gwen's cooking was the cause of Tom's sleeplessness – that and the lack of exercise. Tom had to stay indoors and do crossword puzzles and jigsaw puzzles, and never even answered the door when the milkman came, in case he gave the poor man measles. The only exercise he took was in the kitchen when he was helping his aunt to cook those large, rich meals – larger and richer than Tom had ever known before.

Tom had few ideas on the causes and cures of sleeplessness, and it never occurred to him to complain. At first he tried to read himself to sleep with Aunt Gwen's schoolgirl stories. They did not even bore him enough for that; but he persevered with them. Then Uncle Alan had found him still reading at half-past eleven at night. There had been an outcry. After that Tom was rationed to ten minutes reading in bed; and he had to promise not to switch the bedroom light on again after it had been switched off and his aunt had bidden him good night. He did not regret the reading, but the dragging hours seemed even longer in the dark.

Philippa Pearce from *Tom's Midnight Garden* (Oxford University Press)

 Answer in sentences.

1   What were the two reasons why Tom could not sleep? *(2 marks)*

2   What is the difference between sleeping and dozing? *(2 marks)*

3   Why was Uncle Alan so cross when he found Tom still reading in bed late at night? *(2 marks)*

4   How did Tom feel about not being allowed to read in bed for more than ten minutes? *(2 marks)*

5   How did Tom spend his days at Aunt Gwen's? *(2 marks)*

6   Why wasn't he allowed to go outdoors and meet people? *(1 mark)*

7   Which sound did Tom get used to hearing during the night? *(1 mark)*

8   Which word best describes how Tom felt at Aunt Gwen's? *(1 mark)*
    lazy   bored   hungry   greedy

9   What does "monologue" mean? *(1 mark)*

10   What does "persevere" mean? *(1 mark)*

UNIT

12

Lucy's nightmare

In Lucy's attic bedroom it was still pitch black. But if she had been awake she would have heard a strange sound – a skylark singing high in the darkness above the house. And if she had been standing in the garden, and looking up into the dark sky through binoculars, she might have seen the glowing, flickering body of the lark, far up there, catching the first rays of the sun, that peered at the bird from behind the world.

The lark's song showered down over the dark, dewy fields, over the house roofs, and over the still, wet gardens. But in Lucy's bedroom it mingled with an even stranger sound, a strange, gasping whimper.

Lucy was having a nightmare. In her nightmare, somebody was climbing the creaky attic stair towards her. Then, a hand tried the latch. It was a stiff latch. To open the door, you had to pull the door towards you before you pressed the latch. If you didn't know the trick, it was almost impossible to open the door. The hand in Lucy's nightmare did not seem to know the trick. The latch clicked and rattled but stayed shut.

Then the latch gave a loud clack, and the door swung wide. On her pillow, Lucy became silent. She seemed to have stopped breathing.

For long seconds the bedroom was very dark, and completely silent, except for the faint singing of the skylark.

Then, in her dream, a hand was laid on Lucy's shoulder. She twisted her head and there, in her dream, saw a dreadful thing bending over her. At first, she thought it was a seal, staring at her with black, shining eyes. But how could it be a seal? It looked like a seal covered with black, shiny oil. A seal that had swum through an oil slick and climbed into her attic bedroom and now held her shoulder with its flipper.

But then she saw, on her shoulder, not a flipper but a human hand. And the hand, too, was slimed with black oil. Then Lucy suddenly knew this was not a seal but a girl, like herself, maybe a little bit younger. And the hand began to shake her, and the girl's face began to cry: "Wake up! Oh, wake up! Oh, please wake up!"

She cried those words so loud it was almost a scream, and Lucy did wake up.

She sat up in bed, panting. What a horrible, peculiar dream. She pulled the bedclothes around her, and stared into the darkness towards the door. Was it open? She knew the door had been closed, as every night. But if the door was now open...

Ted Hughes from *The Iron Woman* (Faber & Faber)

 Answer in sentences.

1   In what part of a house is the attic? *(1 mark)*

2   What sounds could be heard in Lucy's bedroom? *(2 marks)*

3   Explain clearly what a nightmare is. *(1 mark)*

4   What sounds did Lucy hear in her nightmare? *(3 marks)*

5   Why would Lucy have needed binoculars to see the lark? *(1 mark)*

6   What sound do you make if you whimper? *(1 mark)*

7   What was it that stopped Lucy whimpering? *(1 mark)*

8   What made the girl in Lucy's nightmare look so dreadful? *(1 mark)*

9   Find the following words in the passage. What other words could be used instead without changing the meaning? *(1 mark each)*

   a) pitch (paragraph 1)
   b) mingled (paragraph 2)
   c) peculiar (last paragraph)

10 The last sentence is not finished because the writer hopes you can guess how it would end. Finish the sentence in your own words to show what Lucy was thinking. *(1 mark)*

   But if the door was now open...

Swans with names

At first sight, one swan looks much like another. If we look at them more closely, however, there is a sure way to tell them apart.

The method of identifying swans was discovered at The Wildfowl Trust, Slimbridge, Gloucestershire, in the west of England. Sir Peter Scott, the famous naturalist, found that he could recognise individual Bewick's swans by the patterns on their bills. He gave the birds names. From then on, it was possible to follow their family life when the swans came back from their breeding-grounds in Siberia every autumn.

Now we know that the pairs stay together for life, and that they live at least 25 years. The parents bring the young swans with them when they leave Siberia.

The family stays together during the first winter. In February they return together to Siberia, flying across Europe. On the way, the swans meet others which have spent the winter in Ireland, or elsewhere in Britain. They gather in favourite stopping-places, where they can rest and feed before flying on to Siberia.

As they fly from the Netherlands to West Germany and onwards across Eastern Europe, the swans become the responsibility of one country after another. The birds themselves are protected by law everywhere they go, but it is just as important to protect the estuaries and marshes which they need as resting-places on the way.

There are other swans which migrate in a similar way in North America, and they probably share a similar family life. So far, however, nobody has found out how to tell them apart in the same way as is used for the Bewick's swans at the Wildfowl Trust in Slimbridge.

Malcolm Penny from *Animal Kingdom* (Wayland Publishers Ltd)

Write out the sentences that are true. *(15 marks)*

1   Bewick's swans stay with the same partner all their life.

2   Bewick's swans can live for more than twenty-five years.

3   Nobody can tell one Bewick's swan from another just by looking at it.

4   Peter Scott discovered that no two Bewick's swans look exactly alike.

5   Bewick's swans fly all the way to Siberia in February without stopping.

6   It is a crime to injure a swan.

7   Every Bewick's swan in the world spends the winter at Slimbridge.

8   Britain is the only place where swans are protected by law.

9   Bewick's swan eggs hatch out in Siberia.

10   No two Bewick's swans have the same pattern on their beaks.

11   Some swans in North America fly away to spend the winter in a different place.

12   The swans go back to Slimbridge every year because they like to see Sir Peter Scott.

13   Bewick's swans stay with their parents for their first winter.

14   Peter Scott knew the Bewick's swans at Slimbridge well enough to give them names.

15   Bewick's swans spend every summer in Siberia.

UNIT 14

Lady with a lamp

Florence Nightingale was a nurse. In 1854 she went to south Russia to look after the British men who had been injured in the Crimean War. This is the story of what she found when she got there.

"I told you so!" The doctor stood still and took his companion's arm. "That woman thinks she's going to run the whole place!" he said, furiously. "Just listen to her!"

Ahead of them, Florence had stopped at the entrance to one of the biggest wards. Inside there were scores and scores of soldiers, many of them still in the uniforms they had been wearing on the battlefield.

"Why are all these men lying on the floors?" she demanded.

The doctors who were conducting her round the hospital before she set her nurses to work shrugged their shoulders. "What can we do? There are not enough beds for the officers, not to speak of the ordinary soldiers!"

"They will die of cold, even if they don't die of wounds."

"I'm afraid you're quite right, Miss Nightingale. But we can't do anything about it. There aren't enough blankets to keep them warm, and we can't get any more."

"What about operations?"

"We have to do them in the wards, of course."

Florence shuddered. "With all the rest of the sick men looking on?"

"Certainly. There are not enough rooms for the men who are sick. We have none to spare for operating-theatres." The doctor who was speaking looked helpless. "There aren't even any operating-tables. We have to use ordinary ones. Ever since the war began we have been making do with what we can get." He turned back into the corridor. "I will *not* have you arguing with me in front of those men, Miss Nightingale."

"Have you enough anaesthetics?"

"Anaesthetics? We have none at all. When a man has his leg cut off he simply has to grin and bear it."

Florence stopped in the middle of the wet, dirty corridor. Her beautiful face was white. She controlled her voice when she spoke,

but it beat about the doctors like a whip. "I have never heard anything so disgraceful in my life. *Why* is everything in this state?" she demanded. "*Why* are there no anaesthetics? *Why* aren't the wards and corridors scrubbed? *Why* haven't these wounded men got clean clothes? *Why* must they lie in the filthy uniforms and muddy blankets they wore in the battlefields?"

The doctors waited for their chief to answer.

When he did so his voice, too, was calm, though he looked as red as the uniform he wore. "Miss Nightingale," he said, "you are a woman. You know nothing about war or about the army. That is why we didn't want you or your nurses here. We knew you would do nothing but criticise. It is impossible to expect women to put up with conditions like these. I admit that. *We're* used to it. You'd better get your nurses together and take the first ship back to England that you can find." He turned on his heel, and began to walk away, but Florence's next words brought him to a stop.

"I am *not* going back to England," she said clearly. "And I do not propose to put up with these conditions. I have been sent by the Government to superintend the nursing of these wounded and sick men, and I am going to start *now*." ▷

"But..." began the doctor, while his colleagues stared at her.

"Have you any soldiers who can scrub floors?" she asked, without waiting for him to finish.

"Scrub? Yes, I suppose so. But we haven't any scrubbing brushes."

"And no money to buy any," put in another doctor. "That's why there is all this confusion. That's why there are no blankets or operating-tables. The Army won't give us money to buy them."

Florence's answer took their breath away. "*I* have the money, gentlemen," she said. "We won't worry about the Army."

"But..." began one of the officers again.

Florence cut in on his question. "Don't you realise that people in England have been giving money to provide comforts for these men? And that I collected a great deal myself?" She did not tell them she had £30,000 to spend as she found necessary. "I want two or three men to come with me into Constantinople to buy scrubbing brushes. Two hundred should be enough to begin with, don't you think?"

Cyril Davey from *Lady with a Lamp* (The Lutterworth Press)

 Choose the correct answer to each question and write it out.
(1.5 marks each)

1 What was Florence Nightingale's reaction to what she saw?

a) It was just what she expected.
b) She was horrified and angry.
c) She was very understanding.

2 What did the doctors think about Florence Nightingale coming to work at the hospital?

a) They thought she was going to be a nuisance.
b) They were grateful for her help.
c) They were relieved she was there.

3   Why did operations take place in the wards in front of all the other patients?

    a) The patients liked to see what was happening.
    b) There was nowhere else to go.
    c) It saved time.

4   What kind of hospital was this one?

    a) It was a hospital just for ordinary soldiers.
    b) It was a hospital just for officers.
    c) It was a hospital for the Army.

5   Why was the hospital so badly equipped?

    a) The doctors were very wasteful.
    b) The Army wouldn't give any money to buy equipment.
    c) The Government thought the hospital didn't need any more equipment.

6   Why were the patients still wearing their filthy uniforms?

    a) They were too ill to be undressed.
    b) They didn't want to wear any other clothes.
    c) There were no clean clothes for them to wear.

7   Which set of adjectives best describes conditions in the hospital?

    a) busy, noisy and damp
    b) untidy, cosy and homely
    c) overcrowded, dirty and cold

8   Florence Nightingale had £30,000 to spend on whatever was necessary. Where did the money come from?

    a) It came from the Government in Britain.
    b) It came from the Army.
    c) It came from the general public in England.

9   What did Florence Nightingale decide to buy first?

    a) scrubbing brushes
    b) blankets
    c) beds

10   Why did Florence Nightingale come to the hospital?

    a) She came to report on conditions.
    b) She came to be in charge of all the nursing care.
    c) She came to make sure that the hospital was clean.

UNIT 15

Sumitra's story

The day before Aunt Leela got married, Mr Patel took Sumitra to Kampala to buy fireworks. Bap always bought the fireworks. He had become something of an expert in staging a display. He knew the names of all the different brands and would spend hours poring over catalogues and working out dramatic colour effects.

"It is important," he told his daughter as the bus jolted on, "to provide the correct balance. Would you, for example, send up a Golden Glory after a Golden Peacock?"

"No, Bap," Sumitra answered dutifully, staring out of the dusty windows at the dry countryside.

"No!" echoed her father, pleased. "You need a Purple Plunderer, an Emerald Emperor, a Blue Bomber to give the right variety and atmosphere." He murmured the names of the fireworks again, savouring the sounds and the images they evoked. They conjured up visions of the Gujarat province where he had been born: temples, peacocks, flowers all touched with the hidden passion and mystery of India.

"And not only colour, but pacing is important," he continued, underlining his message with an outstretched finger. "First a quick rocket, to lift the eyes, then an action firework exploding in the middle distance, then some fire crackers, for excitement!" Sumitra had heard it all before. She leant back drowsily on the hard seat and let Bap ramble on.

There were five coins in her cotton purse and they rattled faintly every time the bus jolted over the bumpy road. She loved the long journey across the sun-baked land. They passed through villages where Indian women crouched outside the houses, making *chapattis* in the sun. They went by African townships where naked children shouted and played outside the huts. Occasionally, high on the hills, they caught a glimpse of the white homes of the British. Here and there waterfalls cascaded down the slopes, running into lakes in which African boys were bathing while women washed clothes.

Bap reread his well-thumbed brochure. "Scarlet Pimpernel, Amber Adventurer, Silver Streak," he intoned. He wanted the celebrations for his sister Leela to be a success.

Rukshana Smith from *Sumitra's Story* (Pan Macmillan Ltd)

 Answer in sentences.

1 Why was Mr Patel buying fireworks? *(1 mark)*

2 What does "poring over catalogues" mean? *(1 mark)*

3 What did Sumitra call her father? *(1 mark)*

4 Which word in the passage means "sleepily"? *(1 mark)*

5 Which of the following items was not a firework in Mr Patel's catalogue?
(1 mark)

   Coral Cascade   **Golden Glory**   **Purple Plunderer**

6 What does "a well-thumbed brochure" mean? *(2 marks)*

7 What relation was Mr Patel to Leela? *(1 mark)*

8 What did Mr Patel mean when he said, "Pacing is important"? *(2 marks)*

9 What do you find out about the place where this passage is set?
Describe the place in your own words. *(3 marks)*

10 Mr Patel was "something of an expert" at arranging firework displays.
What does this mean? *(2 marks)*

Black Beauty

The name of the coachman was John Manly. He had a wife and one little child and they lived in the coachman's cottage very near the stables.

The next morning he took me into the yard and gave me a good grooming. Just as I was going into my box with my coat soft and bright, the squire came in to look at me, and seemed pleased.

"John," he said, "I meant to have tried the new horse this morning, but I have other business. You may as well take him for a round after breakfast. Go by the common and the Highwood, and come back by the water-mill and the river; that will show his paces."

"I will, sir," said John.

After breakfast he came and fitted me with a bridle. He was very particular in letting out and taking in the straps, to fit my head comfortably. Then he brought in the saddle, but it was not broad enough for my back; he saw this in a moment, and went for another, which fitted nicely. He rode me at first slowly, then at a trot, and afterwards at a canter, and when we were on the common he gave me a light touch with his whip, and we had a splendid gallop.

"Ho, ho! My boy," he said, as he pulled me up, "you would like to follow the hounds, I think."

As we came back through the park we met the Squire and Mrs Gordon walking. They stopped, and John jumped off.

"Well, John, how does he go?"

"First-rate, sir," answered John. "He is as fleet as a deer, and has a fine spirit, too; but the lightest touch of the rein will guide him. Down at the end of the common we met one of those travelling carts hung all over with baskets, rugs and such like. You know, sir, many horses will not pass these carts quietly; but he just took a good look at it, and then went on as quietly and pleasantly as could be.

"Some men were shooting rabbits near the Highwood, and a gun went off close by; he pulled up a little and looked, but did not stir a step to right or left. I just held the rein steady and did not hurry him; it's my opinion he has not been frightened or ill-used while he was young."

"That's well," said the squire. "I will try him myself tomorrow."

The next day I was brought up for my master. I remembered my mother's counsel and my good old master's, and I tried to do exactly what the squire wanted me to do. I found he was a very good rider, and thoughtful for his horse, too. When we came home, the lady was at the hall door as he rode up.

"Well, my dear," she said, "how do you like him?"

"He is exactly what John said, my dear. A pleasanter creature I never wish to mount. What shall we call him?"

"Would you like Ebony?" said she; "he is as black as ebony."

"No; not Ebony."

"Will you call him Blackbird, like your uncle's old horse?"

"No; he is far handsomer than old Blackbird ever was."

"Yes," she said, "he is really quite a beauty, and he has such a sweet, good-tempered face and such a fine, intelligent eye – what do you say to calling him Black Beauty?"

"Black Beauty – why, yes, I think that is a very good name. If you like, it shall be so." And that is how I got my name. ⇨

Anna Sewell from *Black Beauty*
(Armada Books)

Answer in sentences.

1 How can you tell from the way he fitted Black Beauty with a bridle and saddle that the coachman was a kind man? *(2 marks)*

2 The coachman praised Black Beauty for four of the reasons below. Write down the four things he said. *(2 marks)*

   a) He can gallop well.
   b) He can jump well.
   c) He is obedient.
   d) He is brave.
   e) He has been well trained.
   f) He has excellent eyesight.

3 Write down everything you learn about Black Beauty's appearance. *(2 marks)*

4 What did Black Beauty think of his new owner, Squire Gordon? *(1 mark)*

5 How can you tell that John Manly, the coachman, was one of Squire Gordon's servants? (Think about the way he speaks and behaves with him.) *(2 marks)*

6 Who is the narrator (the one telling the story) in this passage? *(1 mark)*

7 What were the three names that Mrs Gordon suggested for her husband's new horse? *(1 mark)*

8 Which one of the three names would you have chosen? Why? *(2 marks)*

9 What does "ill-used" mean? *(1 mark)*

10 What does "counsel" mean? *(1 mark)*

The cloth of emperors

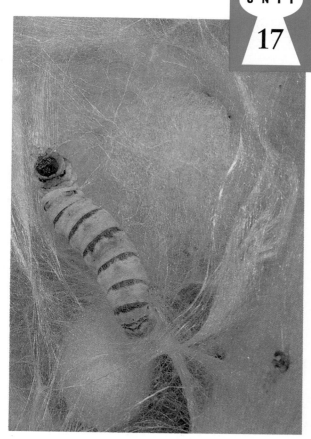

Kings and princes have used it to make
their clothes and decorate their houses
for hundred of years. And it is made by
a tiny caterpillar. What is it? It is silk,
an ancient material which came from
China and has been woven into rugs,
clothes, tapestries and decorations of
all kinds for close to 4,000 years. It is a
rich, soft shining cloth, lovely to wear
and beautiful to see.

Where does silk come from? How
is it made?

Silk is a natural material made
from tiny threads that are squeezed out
as a liquid, from the body of the
silkworm. The silkworm is not really a
worm at all but a caterpillar. The liquid
silk comes out of its body at about 30
centimetres a minute, and it hardens when it touches the air. It is
what the caterpillar uses to form its cocoon. Inside the egg-shaped
ball of rich material, which is waterproof, the caterpillar takes two
weeks to become a moth. The moth spits out a substance that breaks
down the cocoon and finds its way outside to mate, lay eggs and die
in two to three days. The problem is, this substance spoils the cocoon
for making silk. So the caterpillars in the cocoon that are used for
silk making have to be stifled with steam or hot air. This is the only
way to make sure that an unbroken thread of silk can be unravelled
from the cocoon.

Silk remained a Chinese secret for hundreds of years. The Chinese
knew how to feed the silkworms on the leaves of the mulberry tree.
They knew how to pluck, chop and prepare the mulberry leaves so
the greedy larvae would eat them. They knew what things to do and
not to do so as to ensure that the worms spin threads of the finest
silk. Here are some old Chinese rules for rearing silkworms. They are
still observed. ⊳

1 A freshly hatched silkworm can be upset by the bark of a dog, the crow of a cock or even a bad smell. These must be avoided.

2 Worms should rest on dry mattresses. They must sleep, eat and work in harmony.

3 If a newly hatched worm is drowsy, tickle it with a chicken feather to help it grow.

4 The attendant to the worms, also called the silkworm mother, should wear clean, simple clothes and should have no strong smells.

The Chinese guarded the secret of how to raise the silkworm for a long time. By law of the emperor, anyone who disclosed the secret would be tortured to death.

Eventually other countries discovered how to grow silkworms. Some stories say that the Roman Emperor Justinian in the sixth century sent monks to China to steal the silkworm eggs. They brought them to Constantinople in hollow canes and after that fine silks were made in the palace there.

Whether the story is true or not, Europeans did learn to make silk, and towns in Italy and France become important for making silk and weaving the finest garments from it. They continue to do so today, along with countries like India, Japan and Nigeria where the art of sericulture has been known for much longer.

It takes 110 cocoons of silk to make a tie, 630 to make a blouse and 3,000 to make a Japanese kimono. Those 3,000 worms eat 60 kilos of mulberry leaves in order to spin the silk needed for the kimono. It is a lot of hard, painstaking work for worms and people.

adapted from *New Caribbean Junior Reader 4* (Ginn & Company)

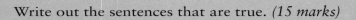 **Write out the sentences that are true.** *(15 marks)*

1   The silkworm is not a worm.

2   The silk is liquid when it first comes out of a silkworm's body.

3   No water can get into the cocoon.

4   A silkworm hatches into a silkmoth after six weeks in the cocoon.

5   If human beings are going to use the silk of the cocoon, they must kill the silkworm.

6   Silkworms love mulberries chopped up very small.

7   The silkmoth lives for only a few days after she has laid her eggs.

8   Over one hundred silkworms are needed to produce enough silk to make a tie.

9   Silk is made in some European countries today.

10 It takes 630 cocoons of silk to make a blouse.

11 Tiny clean clothes are made for the silkmoths after they have laid their eggs.

12 Every newly hatched silkworm has to be gently tickled with a chicken feather or it won't grow.

13 The only country where silk has never been made is America.

14 Silkworms don't like strong smells.

15 It is not very quick or easy to make silk.

The bully asleep

One afternoon, when grassy
Scents through the classroom crept,
Bill Craddock laid his head
Down on his desk, and slept.

The children came round him:
Jimmy, Roger, and Jane;
They lifted his head timidly
And let it sink again.

"Look, he's gone sound asleep, Miss,"
Said Jimmy Adair:
"He stays up all the night, you see;
His mother doesn't care."

"Stand away from him, children."
Miss Andrews stooped to see.
"Yes, he's asleep; go on
With your writing, and let him be."

"Now's a good chance!" whispered Jimmy;
And he snatched Bill's pen and hid it.
"Kick him under the desk, hard;
He won't know who did it."

"Fill all his pockets with rubbish –
Paper, apple-cores, chalk."
So they plotted, while Jane
Sat wide-eyed at their talk.

Not caring, not hearing,
Bill Craddock he slept on;
Lips parted, eyes closed –
Their cruelty gone.

"Stick him with pins!" muttered Roger.
"Ink down his neck!" said Jim.
But Jane, tearful and foolish,
Wanted to comfort him.

John Walsh from *The Puffin Book of Children's 20th Century Verse*
ed. Brian Patten (Puffin Books)

 **Answer in sentences.**

1   What was the name of the bully who was asleep? *(1 mark)*

2   What does the word "timidly" (verse 2) tell us about how the children felt when they lifted up his head and let it sink back on the desk again? *(2 marks)*

3   Why was the bully so tired? *(2 marks)*

4   What did Jimmy do to get his own back on the bully? *(2 marks)*

5   Why did the boys think it would be a good opportunity to kick him hard even though it would wake him up? *(2 marks)*

6   Write down four acts of revenge that they discuss and plan but don't actually carry out before the end of the poem. *(2 marks)*

7   Why was Jane "wide-eyed" at the boys' talk? *(2 marks)*

8   Why do you think Jane wanted to comfort Bill Craddock? *(2 marks)*

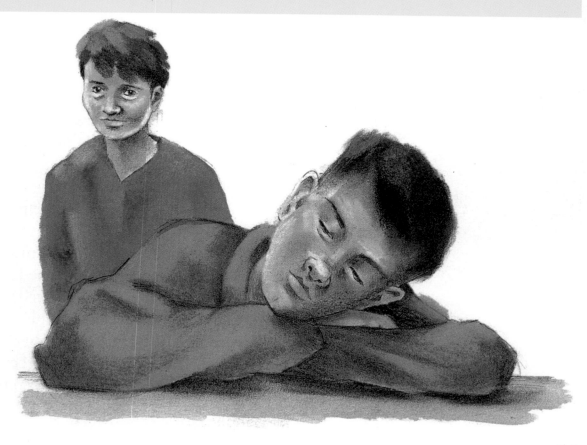

The chicken gave it to me

Andrew laid it on Gemma's desk. A cloud of farmyard dust puffed up in her face. The first thing she asked when she stopped sneezing was:

"Where did you get that?"

"The chicken gave it to me."

"What chicken? How could a chicken give it to you? It's a *book*."

It was, too. A tiny little book. The cover was just a bit of old farm sack with edges that looked as if they had been – yes, well – *pecked*. And the writing was all thin and scratchy and – there's no way round this – *chickeny*.

"This is ridiculous! Chickens can't write books. Chickens can't *read*."

"The chicken gave it to me," Andrew repeated helplessly.

"But *how*?"

So Andrew told her how he'd been walking past the fence that ran round the farm sheds, and suddenly this chicken had leaped out in front of him in the narrow pathway.

"Pounced on me, really."

"Don't be silly, Andrew. Chickens don't pounce."

"This one did," Andrew said stubbornly. "It fluttered and squawked and made the most tremendous fuss. I was quite frightened. And it kept pushing this book at me with its scabby little foot – just pushing the book towards me whichever way I stepped. The chicken was absolutely determined I should take it."

Gemma sat back in her desk and stared. She stared at Andrew as if she'd never even seen him before, as if they hadn't been sharing a desk for weeks and weeks, borrowing each other's rubbers, getting on one another's nerves, telling each other secrets. She thought she knew him well. Had he gone mad?

"Have you gone *mad*?"

Andrew leaned closer and hissed rather fiercely in her ear.

"Listen," he said. "I didn't *choose* to do this, you know. I didn't *want* this to happen. I didn't get out of bed this morning and fling back the curtains and say to myself, 'Heigh-ho! What a great day to walk to school down the path by the farm sheds, minding my own business, and get attacked by some ferocious hen who has decided I am the one to read his wonderful book – ' "

"Her wonderful book," interrupted Gemma. "Hens aren't him. They're all her. That's how they get to lay eggs."

Andrew chose to ignore this.

"Well," he said. "That's what happened. Believe me or don't believe me. I don't care. I'm simply telling you that this chicken stood there making a great fuss and kicking up a storm until I reached down to pick up her dusty little book. Then she calmed down and strolled off."

"Not strolled, Andrew," Gemma said. "Chickens don't stroll. She may have strutted off. Or even – "

But Andrew had shoved his round little face right up close to Gemma's, and he was hissing again.

"Gemma! This is *important*. Don't you *see*?"

And, all at once, Gemma believed him. Maybe she'd gone mad too. She didn't know. But she didn't think Andrew was making it up, and she didn't think Andrew was dreaming.

The chicken gave it to him.

She picked it up. More dust puffed out as, carefully, she stretched the sacking cover flat on her desk to read the scratchy chicken writing of the title.

The True Story of Harrowing Farm

Opening it to the first page, she slid the book until it was exactly halfway between the two of them.

Together they began to read.   ⇨

Anne Fine from *The Chicken Gave It to Me* (Egmont Books)

1   What made the book look as if a chicken had made it and written it? *(2 marks)*

2   Explain exactly how Andrew must have been feeling when he repeated helplessly that a chicken had given the book to him. *(2 marks)*

3   What is the difference between strolling and strutting? *(1 mark)*

4   Find the following words in the passage. What other words or phrases could be used instead without changing the meaning? *(1 mark each)*

   a) ridiculous (paragraph 6)
   b) ferocious (paragraph 16)
   c) ignore (paragraph 18)

5   Several words are used in the passage that are to do with different ways of saying something. Explain clearly the special meaning of the following words. *(1 mark each)*

   a) repeat
   b) interrupt
   c) hiss

6   Why did Gemma believe Andrew in the end? Explain what was convincing about the way Andrew told his story. *(2 marks)*

7   What do you find out about what Gemma's personality is like from this passage? Include all the details you can find. *(2 marks)*

Treasure hunting

Bottle dumps

Digging your way through a hundred year old rubbish dump
does not sound as exciting as using a metal detector. Your
treasure will be made up of bottles, stone ginger-beer jars
and the china lids from old pots of shaving cream and
toothpaste, rather than gold or silver coins. But if you can
pinpoint a single dump which has not already been dug, you
may find yourself digging up hundreds of beautiful bottles
and pot lids.

Why dig for bottles?

Bottles come in a fascinating variety of shapes and many
brilliant colours. Keen collectors in Britain, America, South
Africa and Australia pay very high prices for rare specimens.

With a metal detector, there is always a chance of finding
a hoard of ancient coins. But there are a lot more
undiscovered bottle dumps around than there are pots of
gold pieces.

Historic rubbish

A hundred years ago, there were no dustmen, except in the
main towns. In the country, the only way to get rid of
rubbish was to dig a pit a little way from the house (and
preferably downwind of it) and dump it there. Every house
of any size had its own dump. There was no tinned or
frozen food and almost everything, from boot polish and
hair grease to meat extract, was sold in bottles or pots.

Each family must have thrown away hundreds of these
every year, so it is no exaggeration to say that even a small
private dump could yield a thousand or more bottles.

Major sites

In large towns, there was already an organized rubbish
collection service. The waste was taken in carts to tips
outside the town or loaded on to barges and taken several
miles away. If you locate one of these big dumps, it could
keep you busy for months on end. ➪

The beauty of bottles

A good collection of bottles and stoneware can be incredibly
beautiful. The range of shapes, colours and sizes – from delicate
ink bottles to sturdy pop and beer bottles – is much greater than
most people realise. Two of the most famous collector's items are
the chunky torpedo-shaped Hamilton and the Codd, which had a
marble trapped in the neck as a stopper. They were both used for
fizzy drinks.

Cleaning up your finds

When to start cleaning

Never clean bottles for at least a day after you dig them up. When
they are buried, stresses and strains are set up in the glass, because
of the damp and the weight of earth pressing down on them.
Glass is actually a very slow-moving liquid and your bottles will
soon re-adjust to the release of pressure. But if you try to clean
them straight away, they will probably shatter.

Outside dirt

This can often be loosened by thrusting the bottle into a bucket of
soft sand and twisting it in different directions. The sand scours
the glass clean.

Cleaning inside

Soak the bottle in lukewarm water and then use a small bottle brush. You can make one by cutting a strip from a spiky nylon hair roller and fixing it to a piece of cane. If there are corners that still will not come clean, put some gravel in the bottle and fill it halfway with water. Place your thumb over the end and shake vigorously.

Stains

Remove stains by rubbing with lemon juice or vinegar and then rinsing thoroughly. Badly stained bottles should be soaked for at least 48 hours in a bucket of water with half a kilo of washing soda dissolved in it.

Ian Elliott Shircore from *Treasure Hunting* (Macdonald Educational Books)

 Write out the sentences that are true. *(15 marks)*

1 Metal detectors can help you find bottles and jars quickly.

2 There are more undiscovered bottle dumps than secret hoards of buried coins.

3 Some people collect bottles.

4 There were no dustmen a hundred years ago.

5 Toothpaste used to be sold in pots with china lids.

6 You can clean the outside of bottles in a bucket of sand.

7 Bottles can be worth a lot of money.

8 Lukewarm water can scald you.

9 You can use lemon juice to remove some stains.

10 Rubbish dumps used to be as close to houses as possible.

11 There could be a thousand bottles in some small rubbish dumps.

12 You can damage bottles you dig up if you wash them right away.

13 Some lemonade bottles used to have marbles instead of corks.

14 Country people used to bury their rubbish.

15 All old bottles are made of green glass.

The Borrowers

"Why so quiet, child?" asked Mrs May one day, when Kate was sitting hunched and idle upon the hassock. "What's the matter with you? Have you lost your tongue?"

"No," said Kate, pulling at her shoe button, "I've lost the crochet hook..." (they were making a bed quilt – in woollen squares: there were thirty still to do), "I know where I put it," she went on hastily; "I put it on the bottom shelf of the book-case just beside my bed."

"On the bottom shelf?" repeated Mrs May, her own needle flicking steadily in the firelight. "Near the floor?"

"Yes," said Kate, "but I looked on the floor. Under the rug. Everywhere. The wool was still there though. Just where I'd left it."

"Oh dear," exclaimed Mrs May lightly, "don't say they're in this house too!"

"That what are?" asked Kate.

"The Borrowers," said Mrs May, and in the half light she seemed to smile.

Kate stared a little fearfully. "Are there such things?" she asked after a moment.

"As what?"

Kate blinked her eyelids. "As people, other people, living in a house who ... borrow things?"

Mrs May laid down her work. "What do you think?" she asked.

"I don't know," said Kate, looking away and pulling hard at her shoe button. "There can't be. And yet" – she raised her head – "and yet sometimes I think there must be."

"Why do you think there must be?" asked Mrs May.

"Because of all the things that disappear. Safety-pins for instance. Factories go on making safety-pins, and every day people go on buying safety-pins and yet, somehow, there never is a safety-pin just when you want one. Where are they all? Now at this minute? Where do they go to? Take needles," she went on. "All the needles my mother ever bought – there must be hundreds – can't just be lying about this house."

"Not lying about the house, no," agreed Mrs May.

"And all the other things we keep on buying. Again and again and again. Like pencils and match-boxes and sealing-wax and hair-slides and drawing-pins and thimbles – "

"And hat-pins," put in Mrs May, "and blotting-paper."

"Yes, blotting paper," agreed Kate, "but not hat-pins."

"That's where you're wrong," said Mrs May, and she picked up her work again. "There was a reason for hat-pins."

Kate stared. "A reason?" she repeated. "I mean – what kind of a reason?"

"Well, there were two reasons really. A hat-pin is a very useful weapon and" – Mrs May laughed suddenly – "but it all sounds such nonsense and" – and she hesitated – "it was so very long ago!"

"But tell me," said Kate, "tell me how you know about the hat-pin. Did you ever see one?"

Mrs May threw her a started glance. "Well, yes – " she began.

"Not a hat-pin," exclaimed Kate impatiently, "a – whatever-you-called-them – a Borrower?"

Mrs May drew a sharp breath. "No," she said quickly, "I never saw one." ▷

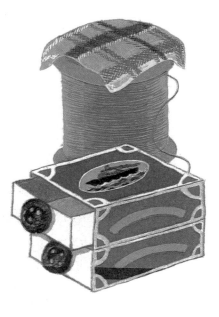

"But someone else saw one," cried Kate, "and you know about it. I can see you do!"

"Hush," said Mrs May, "no need to shout!" She gazed downwards at the upturned face and then she smiled and her eyes slid away into distance. "I had a brother – " she began uncertainly.

Kate knelt upon the hassock. "And he saw them!"

"I don't know," said Mrs May, shaking her head. "I just don't know!" She smoothed out her work upon her knee. "He was such a tease. He told us so many things – my sister and me – impossible things. He was killed," she added gently, "many years ago now on the North-West Frontier. He became a colonel of his regiment. He died what they call 'a hero's death'…"

"Was he your only brother?"

"Yes, and he was our little brother. I think that was why" – she thought for a moment, still smiling to herself – "yes, why he told us such impossible stories, such strange imaginings. He was jealous, I think, because we were older – and because we could read better. He wanted to impress us; he wanted, perhaps, to shock us. And yet" – she looked into the fire – "there was something about him – perhaps because we were brought up in India among mystery and magic and legend – something that made us think that he saw things that other people could not see; sometimes we'd know he was teasing, but at other times – well, we were not so sure…" She leaned forward and, in her tidy way, brushed a fan of loose ashes under the grate, then, brush in hand, she stared again at the fire. "He wasn't a very strong little boy: the first time he came home from India he got rheumatic fever. He missed a whole term of school and was sent away to the country to get over it. To the house of a great-aunt. Later I went there myself. It was a strange old house…" She hung up the brush on its brass hook and, dusting her hands on her handkerchief, she picked up her work. "Better light the lamp," she said.

"Not yet," begged Kate, leaning forward. "Please go on. Please tell me – "

"But I've told you."

"No you haven't. This old house – wasn't that where he saw – he saw...?"

Mrs May laughed. "Where he saw the Borrowers? Yes, that's what he told us... what he'd have us believe. And, what's more, it seems that he didn't just see them but that he got to know them very well; that he became part of their lives, as it were; in fact, you might almost say that he became a Borrower himself..."

Mary Norton from *The Borrowers* (Odyssey Classics)

Answer in sentences *(1.5 marks each)*

1   How did Kate feel at the beginning of the passage?

2   What is a hassock?

3   What did Mrs May think had happened to all the needles that Kate's mother had lost?

4   What made Kate believe that the Borrowers must exist?

5   Where did Mrs May live when she was a little girl?

6   How did Mrs May's brother die?

7   Did Mrs May think her brother had been telling the truth about the Borrowers?

8   Why might her brother have made up the stories?

9   How did Mrs May feel when she talked about her brother?

10   Why didn't Kate want the lamp to be lit?

The longest journey in the world

"Last one into bed
has to switch out the light."
It's just the same every night.
There's a race.
I'm ripping off my trousers and shirt –
he's kicking off his shoes and socks.

"My sleeve's stuck."
"This button's too big for its button-hole."
"Have you hidden my pyjamas?"
"Keep your hands off mine."
If you win
you get where it's safe
before the darkness comes –
but if you lose
if you're last
you know what you've got coming up is
the journey from the light switch
to your bed.
It's the Longest Journey in the World.

"You're last tonight," my brother says.
And he's right.
There is nowhere so dark
as that room in the moment
after I've switched out the light.

There is nowhere so full of dangerous things –
things that love dark places –
things that breathe only when you breathe
and hold their breath when I hold mine.
So I have to say:
"I'm not scared."
That face, grinning in the pattern on the wall
isn't a face –
"I'm not scared."

That prickle on the back of my neck
is only the label on my pyjama jacket –
"I'm not scared."
That moaning-moaning is nothing
but water in a pipe –
"I'm not scared."

Everything's going to be just fine
as soon as I get into that bed of mine.
Such a terrible shame
it's always the same
it takes so long
it takes so long
it takes so long
to get there.

From the light switch
to my bed.
It's the Longest Journey in the World.

Michael Rosen from *Touchstones I* ed. Michael and Peter Benton (Hodder and Stoughton)

Answer in sentences.

1   What was the game that the two boys played every night? *(2 marks)*

2   Why was it so frightening to be the loser? *(2 marks)*

3   Why was it so wonderful to be the winner? *(2 marks)*

4   Which verbs in the first verse suggest undressing very quickly? *(2 marks)*

5   What caused the moaning-moaning sound that could be heard in the room?
    (1 mark)

6   What was the boy really thinking each time he said, "I'm not scared"?
    (2 marks)

7   What do you think the boy was doing while he said:
    "it takes so long / it takes so long / it takes so long"? *(2 marks)*

8   What do you think the boy did at the words "to get there"? *(2 marks)*

UNIT 23

Loll's first day

The morning came, without any warning, when my sisters surrounded me, wrapped me in scarves, tied up my boot-laces, thrust a cap on my head, and stuffed a baked potato in my pocket.

"What's this?" I said.

"You're starting school today."

"I ain't. I'm stopping 'ome."

"Now, come on, Loll. You're a big boy now."

"I ain't."

"You are."

"Boo-hoo."

They picked me up bodily, kicking and bawling, and carried me up to the road.

"Boys who don't go to school get put into boxes, and turn into rabbits, and get chopped up Sundays."

I felt this was overdoing it rather, but I said no more after that. I arrived at the school just three feet tall and fatly wrapped in my scarves. The playground roared like a rodeo, and the potato burned through my thigh. Old boots, ragged stockings, torn trousers and skirts, went skating and skidding around me. The rabble closed in; I was encircled; grit flew in my face like shrapnel. Tall girls with frizzled hair, and huge boys with sharp elbows, began to prod me with hideous interest. They plucked at my scarves, spun me round like a top, screwed my nose and stole my potato.

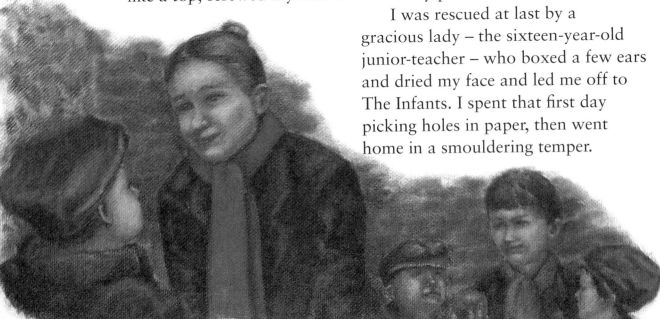

I was rescued at last by a gracious lady – the sixteen-year-old junior-teacher – who boxed a few ears and dried my face and led me off to The Infants. I spent that first day picking holes in paper, then went home in a smouldering temper.

"What's the matter, Loll? Didn't he like it at school, then?"

"They never gave me the present!"

"Present? What present?"

"They said they'd give me a present."

"Well, now, I'm sure they didn't."

"They did! They said: 'You're Laurie Lee, ain't you? Well, just you sit there for the present.' I sat there all day but I never got it. I ain't going back there again!"

But after a week I felt like a veteran and grew as ruthless as anyone else.

Laurie Lee from *Cider with Rosie* (Vintage)

Answer in sentences.

1   How did Loll feel about starting school? *(1 mark)*

2   Who took him to school? *(1 mark)*

3   Why was he given a baked potato? *(1 mark)*

4   Loll thought the story about boys who didn't go to school was "overdoing it rather". What does this mean? *(2 marks)*

5   Why did the playground "roar like a rodeo"? *(1 mark)*

6   Which of the following words is the plural of "potato"? *(1 mark)*

   potatos   potatoes   potattos

7   What did Loll think it meant when he was told to "sit there for the present"? *(1 mark)*

8   What did "sit there for the present" really mean? *(1 mark)*

9   What sort of a temper is a "smouldering" temper? *(2 marks)*

10 Why did Loll go home in a smouldering temper? *(1 mark)*

11 After a week Loll "felt like a veteran". What does this mean? *(2 marks)*

12 What does "ruthless" mean? *(1 mark)*

UNIT 24

Bad news

"Please'm," she said, "the Master wants you to just step into the study. He looks like the dead, mum; I think he's had bad news. You'd best prepare yourself for the worst, 'm – p'raps it's a death in the family or a bank busted or – "

"That'll do, Ruth," said Mother gently; "you can go." Then Mother went into the library. There was more talking. Then the bell rang again, and Ruth fetched a cab. The children heard boots go out and down the steps. The cab drove away, and the front door shut. Then Mother came in. Her dear face was as white as her lace collar, and her eyes looked very big and shining. Her mouth looked like just a line of pale red – her lips were thin and not their proper shape at all.

"It's bedtime," she said. "Ruth will put you to bed."

"But you promised we should sit up late tonight because Father's come home," said Phyllis.

"Father's been called away – on business," said Mother. "Come, darlings, go at once."

They kissed her and went. Roberta lingered to give Mother an extra hug and to whisper:

"It wasn't bad news, Mammy, was it? Is anyone dead – or –"

"Nobody's dead – no," said Mother, and she almost seemed to push Roberta away. "I can't tell you anything tonight, my pet. Go, dear, go *now*."

So Roberta went.

Ruth brushed the girls' hair and helped them to undress. (Mother almost always did this herself.) When she had turned down the gas and left them she found Peter, still dressed, waiting on the stairs.

"I say, Ruth, what's up?" he asked.

"Don't ask me no questions and I won't tell you no lies," the red-headed Ruth replied. "You'll know soon enough."

Later that night Mother came up and kissed all three children as they lay asleep. But Roberta was the only one whom the kiss woke, and she lay mousey-still, and said nothing.

"If Mother doesn't want us to know she's been crying," she said to herself as she heard through the dark the catching of her Mother's breath, "we *won't* know it. That's all."

When they came down to breakfast the next morning, Mother had already gone out.

"To London," Ruth said, and left them to their breakfast.

"There's something awful the matter," said Peter, breaking his egg. "Ruth told me last night we should know soon enough."

"Did you *ask* her?" said Roberta, with scorn.

"Yes, I did!" said Peter, angrily. "If you could go to bed without caring whether Mother was worried or not, I couldn't. So there."

"I don't think we ought to ask the servants things Mother doesn't tell us," said Roberta.

"That's right, Miss Goody-Goody," said Peter, "preach away."

"*I'm* not goody," said Phyllis, "but I think Bobbie's right this time."

"Of course. She always is. In her own opinion," said Peter.

"Oh, *don't!*" cried Roberta, putting down her egg-spoon; "don't let's be horrid to each other. I'm sure some dire calamity is happening. Don't let's make it worse!"

E. Nesbit from *The Railway Children* (Puffin Books)

 Answer in sentences.

1 Why did Ruth call the children's father "the Master"? *(1 mark)*

2 When Mother came back into the room, how could the children tell that she had heard some dreadful news? *(3 marks)*

3 "Roberta lingered to give Mother an extra hug".
   What does "lingered" mean? *(1 mark)*

4 How could Roberta tell that her mother had been crying when she came to kiss them goodnight? *(2 marks)*

5 Roberta was the oldest child and Phyllis was the youngest.
   Would you guess this from the way they behave? Why? *(4 marks)*

6 What was Roberta's family nickname? *(1 mark)*

7 What did Peter mean when he called Roberta "Miss Goody-Goody"? *(2 marks)*

8 Roberta was sure that "some dire calamity" was happening.
   What does this mean? *(1 mark)*

Rosie and the Boredom Eater

Rosie Barker was bored. As usual. She had been bored ever since
the Barkers had moved house. The old house had had a garden.
The one they had moved to had only a cobbled yard. None of the
houses in Latimer Street had a garden.

"I'm bored," Rosie told her mother.
"Why can't we have a garden?"

"Because," replied Mrs Barker.

"That's not a proper answer," Rosie told her.

"It's the only one there is. And you can be
bored when you do have a garden, as well as
when you haven't."

"At least there's *company* in a garden," said
Rosie. "Birds and snails and ... centipedes ... and
worms, and things."

"I must say, Rosie," said her mother, "that I
never noticed you playing much with worms."

"At least they're alive," said Rosie
obstinately. "They're company. They wriggle
about."

"Oh, *do* stop going on about worms!"
Mr Barker came in.

"What's all this about worms?" he asked.

"Oh, she reckons she wants some to play
with. She says she's bored."

"She always is," he said. "Why don't you go out, Rosie? Find some
kids to play with. Make some friends."

"If I'd got any brothers and sisters, I wouldn't have to," said Rosie.
Mrs Barker sighed.

"Here we go again!"

"It ought to be against the law to only have one child," Rosie told
them. "There ought to be no such things as onlys. It's cruelty to children."

"There's no point in going over all that again, Rosie," her mother
told her.

"I fought cat and dog with my brother and sister," Mr Barker said.

"At least if you're fighting you're not *bored*!" said Rosie. ⇨

"Listen!" said Mrs Barker. "I don't want to hear that word again today. Do you hear me, Rosie?"

"What word? Bored? You mean you don't want to hear the word bored again? Or do you mean some other word besides bored? You mean you're bored with –"

"Rosie!" Mr Barker warned her.

"I'm going *out*!" said Rosie. "To find a friend!"

She went out the back door and banged it behind her. She went across the little cobbled yard and through the gate that led to the back alley. She looked left and right. She saw only the blank windows of terraced houses, and rows of chimney pots. Even they were lifeless, with not so much as a puff of smoke.

"Where *is* everybody?" she wondered.

Rosie knew that the house next door to hers was empty. She also knew that her parents would not approve of her nosing around it. She did it, just the same. It was the only thing she could think of to do.

"And if I don't do something soon, I might actually *die* of boredom," she told herself. "Here lies the body of Rosie Barker, aged nine, died of boredom."

She lifted the latch of the back gate of number twenty-seven and pushed. It swung slowly open, with the kind of creak you get in a horror film.

Rosie went in and shut the gate behind her. She looked around. As far as she could see, the yard of number twenty-seven was identical to the yard of number twenty-five. Nobody there – no birds, no worms. Just a dustbin.

"Boring boring boring!" she said out loud. "I might as well be sitting in that dustbin with the lid on!"

She stared at the bin. She knew it was empty, because the people next door had moved out weeks ago. It actually occurred to her that to climb inside it and pull the lid on after her might be quite an interesting and unusual thing to do. At least it wouldn't be boring.

Then the dustbin moved. It didn't move forward or backward. It just rocked, ever so slightly.

"Now I'm seeing things!" said Rosie.

She knew, of course, that dustbins don't move. They just stand around waiting to be filled with rubbish.

The dustbin moved again. This time, Rosie was sure she hadn't imagined it. She stood and boggled. Again the dustbin rocked.

Rosie cleared her throat.

"Is there – anybody there?" she asked.

There was no reply. Rosie felt extremely silly, standing there talking to a dustbin.

"Stupid old bin!" she muttered.

Then the dustbin really took off. It began to rock violently, back and forth, back and forth. It was as if there were someone inside there, working it to and fro. It rocked so wildly that its lid began to rattle and threatened to fly right off.

"N-not an earthquake!" thought Rosie Barker. "N-nothing else is jumping. I'm going mad, that's what it is. I've gone mad with boredom!"

At that moment the dustbin lid *did* fly off. It dropped to the cobbles with a clatter. The bin stopped rocking. Silence.

"The thing to do now," thought Rosie, "is to go and see if there's anyone – or anything – inside ..."

Somehow she did not feel much like doing this. ▷

"Just *tiptoe* up," she told herself. "Really pussyfoot up, so that whatever it is won't hear!"

This is what she did. Slowly, slowly she tiptoed forward. It was like playing Grandmother's Footsteps by herself. The dustbin was stock still now, stiff and ordinary as any other dustbin. She was nearly there now. Nearly ... nearly ...

"Eeeech!"

Rosie screamed and nearly jumped out of her skin. There was somebody in the dustbin!

"OOOOEEEH!" quavered Rosie Barker. "Help!"

"What d'ye mean, help?" The voice was high and cracked. "What d'you think I'm *here* for?"

Rosie gasped. She craned forward. All she could see was a pair of skinny hands that seemed to be clasped over a tangle of grey hair. An old, old man must be hunched up in there. It was impossible. She knew it. Nobody's grandfather that *she* knew went hiding themselves in dustbins, all hunched up.

"Well?" the voice snapped, and at the same time the skinny hands flew up, and all at once there was a *face* in the dustbin.

Rosie Barker boggled. She boggled till her eyes nearly popped out. She was looking at the oldest, wickedest face she had ever seen, chalky white and powdery looking. Round it flew a halo of grey hair and beard, all tangled with cobwebs and dust.

"G-good morning!" said Rosie. She said it with extreme politeness. She did not know whether whoever it was had any toes. If it had, she didn't want to tread on them.

No reply. She was being watched by black beady eyes.

"Who are you?"

She was not sure what she expected him to say. Certainly she did not expect him to say "I'm your long lost Uncle Arthur from Australia." She did not even *have* a long lost Uncle Arthur, as far as she knew.

"The Boredom Eater!" The hoarse whisper ran echoing about the bin.

"Boredom Eater?" echoed Rosie blankly.

"Boredom Eater!"

Helen Cresswell from *Rosie and the Boredom Eater* (Heinemann Library)

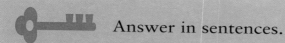
1   Why was Rosie so bored? *(1 mark)*

2   What did Rosie mean when she said "there ought to be no such things as onlys"? *(2 marks)*

3   What was the number of Rosie's new house and the name of the road? *(2 marks)*

4   How could Rosie be sure that the house next door was empty? *(1 mark)*

5   The yard of the house next door was identical to Rosie's yard. What does "identical" mean? *(1 mark)*

6   Explain how Rosie knew that she wasn't in an earthquake when the dustbin started to rock about. *(1 mark)*

7   The old man in the dustbin said that he was there to help Rosie. How do you think he will help her? *(1 mark)*

8   What facts do we learn about Rosie in this passage? (Look for information about her home, her family and her age.) *(2 marks)*

9   What do you find out about what Rosie's personality is like from this passage? Include all the details that you can find. *(3 marks)*

10   What does "quavered" mean? *(1 mark)*

UNIT 26

Newspaper article

HOP-SCOTCH TOTS

Bubbly pals Katy Rodger and Hannah Kamester hop-scotched the length of Exmouth sea front – and raised money for an organisation which has helped keep them alive.

For the four-year-olds suffer from anaphylaxis – a rare but serious food allergy which means to even touch some foods can spark a massive reaction.

Katy was discovered to be severely allergic to dairy products almost from birth but Hannah was two before it was found she had a near identical problem with peanuts.

Although the vigilance of their parents has kept both girls safe they also rely on the Anaphylaxis Campaign – a charity which keeps them up to date on product information and the latest medical breakthroughs.

To say thank-you for their support, on Sunday the Exmouth pair joined forces and hop-scotched from Orcombe Point to the Inshore Lifeboat Station. Together they managed a mile of the sea front and raised £350 in the effort.

Katy's mum, Alison said: "We have to watch them like a hawk at all times because the consequences could be horrific. They both know they must not accept any food from anyone but it is a constant worry that somehow they will eat something that they are allergic to."

Both families have seen the girls suffer anaphylactic shocks either from eating the wrong food or by touching it.

In each case they can swell up, develop rashes and hives, struggle with their breathing and face reactions similar to a burn – both inside and outside the body.

Both girls must carry an adrenaline injection which in an emergency must be pumped into the muscle – something which everyone left in charge of the youngsters must learn how to do.

Kathryn Kamester, Hannah's mother, said: "It is something we just hope never has to be used but it is good to know it is there if we need it."

The families have offered each other support since a chance meeting at the Rainbow Nursery in Exmouth.

But they say the Anaphylaxis Campaign has been a massive help.

The Campaign is fighting for better research into the condition, legislation for improved labelling of foods and the education of medics.

from *The Leader*, 26 October 1994, Exmouth and Budleigh Salterton (local newspaper)

🔑🗝 **Answer in sentences.**

1   How old are Katy and Hannah? *(1 mark)*

2   How far did the girls hop-scotch along Exmouth sea front? *(1 mark)*

3   How much money did they raise? *(1 mark)*

4   What must Katy not eat, drink or touch? *(1 mark)*

5   What must Hannah not eat or touch? *(1 mark)*

6   Their parents have to "watch them like a hawk".
    Why is this a good way of describing how they watch over the girls? *(1 mark)*

7   List three possible allergic reactions the girls might have. *(2 marks)*

8   If one of the girls did have an allergic reaction, what treatment should be
    used immediately? *(1 mark)*

9   How would the improved labelling of food help the girls? *(1 mark)*

10 What do the following words and phrases mean? *(1 mark each)*
    a) **allergy**
    b) **vigilance**
    c) **product information**
    d) **a medical breakthrough**
    e) **legislation**

UNIT 27

The ground gives way

If you went too near the edge of the chalk-pit the ground would give way. Barney had been told this often enough. Everybody had told him. His grandmother, every time he came to stay with her. His sister, every time she wasn't telling him something else. Barney had a feeling, somewhere in his middle, that it was probably true about the ground giving way. But still, there was a difference between being told and seeing it happen. And today was one of those grey days when there was nothing to do, nothing to play, and nowhere to go. Except to the chalk-pit. The dump.

Barney got through the rickety fence and went to the edge of the pit. This had been the side of a hill once, he told himself. Men had come to dig away chalk and left this huge hole in the earth. He thought of all the sticks of chalk they must have made, and all the blackboards in all the schools they must have written on. They must have dug and dug for hundreds of years. And then they got tired of digging, or somebody had told them to stop before they dug away all the hill. And now they did not know what to do with this empty hole and they were trying to fill it up again. Anything people didn't want they threw into the bottom of the pit.

He crawled through the rough grass and peered over. The sides of the pit were white chalk, with lines of flints poking out like bones in places. At the top was crumbly brown earth and the roots of the trees that grew on the edge. The roots looped over the edge, twined in the air and grew back into the earth. Some of the trees hung over the edge, holding on desperately by a few roots. The earth and chalk had fallen away beneath them, and one day they too would fall to the bottom of the pit. Strings of ivy and the creeper called Old Man's Beard hung in the air.

Far below was the bottom of the pit. The dump. Barney could see strange bits of wreckage among the moss and elder bushes and nettles. Was that the steering wheel of a ship? The tail of an aeroplane? At least there was a real bicycle. Barney felt sure he could make it go if only he could get at it. They didn't let him have a bicycle.

Barney wished he was at the bottom of the pit.

And the ground gave way.

Barney felt his head going down and his feet going up. There was a rattle of falling earth beneath him. Then he was falling, still clutching the clump of grass that was falling with him.

"This is what it's like when the ground gives way," thought Barney. Then he seemed to turn a complete somersault in the air, bumped into a ledge of chalk half-way down, crashed through some creepers and ivy and branches, and landed on a bank of moss.

His thoughts did those funny things they do when you bump your head and you suddenly find yourself thinking about what you had for dinner last Tuesday, all mixed up with seven times six. Barney lay with his eyes shut, waiting for his thoughts to stop being mixed up. Then he opened them. ⇨

71

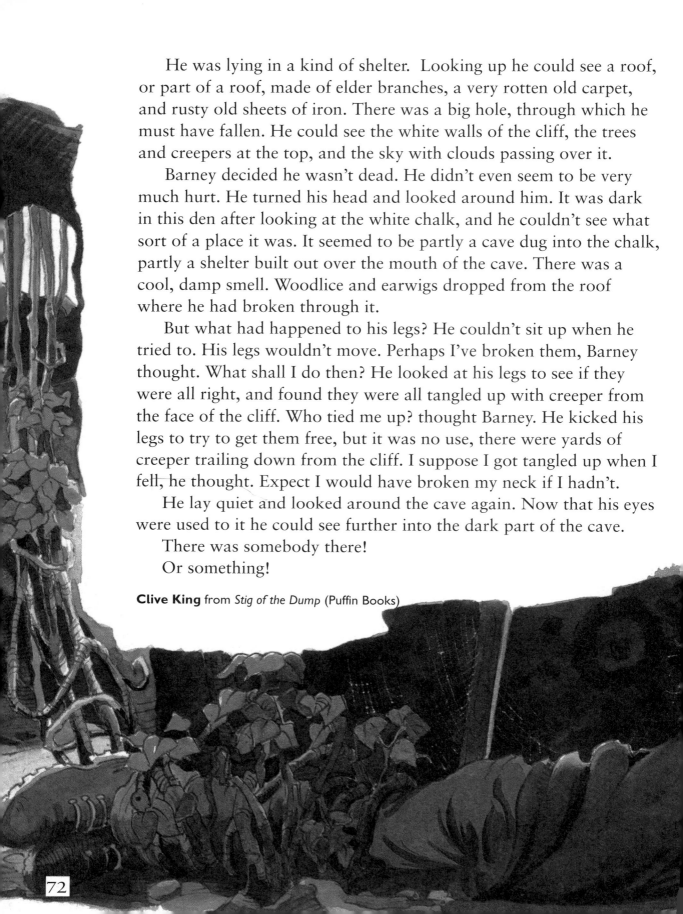

He was lying in a kind of shelter. Looking up he could see a roof, or part of a roof, made of elder branches, a very rotten old carpet, and rusty old sheets of iron. There was a big hole, through which he must have fallen. He could see the white walls of the cliff, the trees and creepers at the top, and the sky with clouds passing over it.

Barney decided he wasn't dead. He didn't even seem to be very much hurt. He turned his head and looked around him. It was dark in this den after looking at the white chalk, and he couldn't see what sort of a place it was. It seemed to be partly a cave dug into the chalk, partly a shelter built out over the mouth of the cave. There was a cool, damp smell. Woodlice and earwigs dropped from the roof where he had broken through it.

But what had happened to his legs? He couldn't sit up when he tried to. His legs wouldn't move. Perhaps I've broken them, Barney thought. What shall I do then? He looked at his legs to see if they were all right, and found they were all tangled up with creeper from the face of the cliff. Who tied me up? thought Barney. He kicked his legs to try to get them free, but it was no use, there were yards of creeper trailing down from the cliff. I suppose I got tangled up when I fell, he thought. Expect I would have broken my neck if I hadn't.

He lay quiet and looked around the cave again. Now that his eyes were used to it he could see further into the dark part of the cave.

There was somebody there!

Or something!

Clive King from *Stig of the Dump* (Puffin Books)

1   Barney's grandmother and sister told him not to go too close to the edge of the chalk-pit. What did they think might happen? *(1 mark)*

2   What evidence in paragraph three shows that the edge of the chalk-pit was dangerous? *(2 marks)*

3   Which word best describes Barney's mood at the beginning of the passage? *(2 marks)*

    frightened   **excited**   **bored**

4   What was the local name for the chalk-pit? *(1 mark)*

5   What was growing at the very bottom of the pit? *(1 mark)*

6   Why did Barney want to have the bicycle at the bottom of the pit? *(2 marks)*

7   Explain in your own words the sound that Barney heard as he fell. *(2 marks)*

8   What was the roof of the shelter made of? *(1 mark)*

9   Why couldn't Barney move his legs? *(2 marks)*

10 What did Barney think could have happened if he hadn't got tangled up in the plants? *(1 mark)*

UNIT 28

I am David

This story is set during the Second World War. David is a prisoner in a concentration camp where he has lived ever since he was a baby. The man in this passage is a cruel prison guard whom David hates. David is astonished when the man tells him that he will help him to escape.

"You must get away tonight," the man had told him. "Stay awake so that you're ready just before the guard's changed. When you see me strike a match, the current will be cut off and you can climb over – you'll have half a minute for it, no more."

In his mind's eye David saw once again the grey bare room he knew so well. He saw the man and was conscious, somewhere in the pit of his stomach, of the hard knot of hate he felt whenever he saw him. The man's eyes were small, repulsive, light in colour, their expression never changing; his face was gross and fat. David had known him all his life, but he never spoke to him more than was barely necessary to answer his questions; and though he had known his name for as long as he could remember, he never said anything but "the man" when he spoke about him or thought of him. Giving him a name would be like admitting that he knew him; it would place him on an equal footing with the others.

But that evening he had spoken to him. He had said, "And if I don't escape?"

The man had shrugged his shoulders. "That'll be none of my business. I have to leave here tomorrow, and whatever my successor may decide to do about you, I shan't be able to interfere. But you'll soon be a big lad, and there's need in a good many places for those strong enough to work."

David knew only too well that those other places would not be any better than the camp where he now was. "And if I get away without being caught, what then?" he had asked.

"Just by the big tree in the thicket that lies on the road out to the mines, you'll find a bottle of water and a compass. Follow the compass southwards till you get to Salonica, and then when no one's looking go on board a ship and hide. You'll have to stay hidden while the ship's at sea, and you'll need the water. Find a ship that's bound for Italy, and when you get there go north till you come to a country called Denmark – you'll be safe there."

Anne Holm from *I am David* (Harcourt)

Answer in sentences.

1 Which words show that David had known the man for a long time? *(2 marks)*

2 What did David hate about the man's eyes? *(2 marks)*

3 Did David know the man's name? *(1 mark)*

4 Did David like the man? *(1 mark)*

5 How would David know that the electricity had been cut off? *(2 marks)*

6 How long would David have to climb over the wall? *(2 marks)*

7 What would David find hidden by the tree? *(2 marks)*

8 Where must David go first? *(1 mark)*

9 When he gets to Salonica, what must he do next? *(1 mark)*

10 Why must David do his best to get to Denmark? *(1 mark)*

UNIT 29

Noise

Noise is measured in units known as decibels (dB). The point at which the average human ear can hear is zero decibels; somewhere around 180 decibels is the lethal level. Rats exposed to levels approaching this turn cannibalistic and eventually die from heart failure.

Sound at 90 decibels or above may cause pain and temporary deafness lasting for minutes or hours. This deafness is a warning that hearing may be damaged permanently unless the source of the noise is removed or unless suitable precautions are taken. Prolonged tinnitus (buzzing in the ears) occurring after a noise has ceased is an indication that some damage has probably occurred.

People who cannot avoid exposure to loud noise (for example, workers using pneumatic drills) should wear ear protection.

Comparative noise levels

jet engine (at 30 metres)		
pneumatic drill (at 1 metre)		
accelerating motor cycle		
food mixer (at 1 metre)		
pop group (at 1.5 metres)		
normal conversation		
whispering		
ticking of a watch		
leaves rustling in the wind		
normal breathing		
decibels (dB)	0 10 20 30 40 50 60 70 80 90 100 110 120 130	

1   Explain in your own words what effect noises of 180 decibels can have on rats.

2   What effect can noises over 90 decibels have on a person?

3   What should workers using pneumatic drills do to protect their ears from the noise?

4   What is the noise level of a pneumatic drill if you are standing one metre away?

5   Which word in the passage means "lasting for a short time"?

6   Which word in the passage means "lasting for ever"?

7   Which word in the passage means "stopped"?

8   Which word in the passage means "injury"?

9   Which word in the passage means "a buzzing in the ears"?

10   What is the decibel level of a normal conversation?

11   What is the decibel level of a ticking watch?

12   Which item in the chart makes a noise of 100 decibels?

13   Which is noisier, the rustling of leaves in the wind or a whisper?

14   Which is noisier, a pop group 1.5 metres away, or an accelerating motor cycle?

15   Which decibel level surprises you most? Why?

UNIT 30

Sam

"Hey Mum, do you know what?"

No answer.

"Hey, Mum."

No answer.

"MUM!"

Sam bellowed with the full force of his lungs. His face turned red as a plum.

"I'm not deaf, dear. There's no need to shout."

Mrs Peach stopped cutting up steak for the dogs' dinner and looked at Sam in the kindly but somehow *unseeing* way she looked at most human beings most of the time. Though she was fond of Sam, she would really have been more interested in him if he had been a dog. Though Sam knew this, he did not resent it – indeed, from his point of view, the situation had its advantages. Other mothers fussed their sons about washing behind their ears and keeping the house tidy. Mrs Peach fussed over her salukis instead: she was too busy grooming them and getting burs out of their coats to worry over such an unimportant thing as a bit of dirt on the back of a boy's neck. As a result, Sam confined his washing activities to as small an area as possible: if he washed his face he stopped short at his jaw line so that he often looked like a dark boy wearing a fair, freckled mask. Today he had omitted even this trifling attention. Looking at him in her abstracted way, Mrs Peach thought he looked exceptionally well and brown.

"What do you want, dear?" she asked.

"I can't remember now."

"You must have wanted something." Mrs Peach tried hard to be a conscientious mother. "Are you hungry, dear?"

"Not specially. We've just had dinner," Sam reminded her.

"Oh, well... Shouldn't you be getting back to school, then?"

"It's Saturday."

"So it is. How silly of me. The vet came yesterday to look at Lady – he always calls on Fridays." She regarded Sam with a perplexed expression. "Saturday... I'm sure there was something I meant to do on Saturday..."

"Shopping? Eggs? Bacon? Baked beans?" Sam spoke with an eye to his stomach. There was always plenty of dog meat and biscuits in the house but other things were liable to run short. "Sunday joint? Vegetables?" There was no answering gleam in Mrs Peach's eye. "Paying the milkman?" Sam suggested.

"He called this morning but I couldn't find my purse."

"Behind the clock on the mantelpiece. If you'd asked me, I'd have told you."

"You weren't here, or I would have done." Mrs Peach ran her fingers through her short hair in the way she did when trying to remember something she had forgotten. (As she was always forgetting something, her hair was nearly as untidy as Sam's.) "Oh well, perhaps I'll remember later," she said, and sighed. ⇨

Sam shifted from one foot to the other. "I'm going out."

"Where are you going?"

"Nowhere."

"Give my regards to Mr Nobody, then," Mrs Peach said, and then added, as Sam reached the door, "I hope 'nowhere' doesn't include Gibbet Wood."

Sam held still for a moment; it struck him that for a vague, forgetful person, his mother often showed uncanny insight. In case he should need to lie, he crossed his fingers in his pocket, but it was all right, his mother just said placidly, "I daresay they'll be out shooting this afternoon, as it's Saturday. I should hate it if someone shot you instead of a pheasant."

Nina Bawden from *The White Horse Gang* (Houghton Mifflin)

 Answer in sentences.

1   Why didn't Mrs Peach answer Sam when he spoke to her at first ? *(1 mark)*

2   What is the difference between speaking and bellowing? *(2 marks)*

3   Why did Sam look so brown? *(1 mark)*

4   How did Mrs Peach know that Sam was right when he said that it was Saturday? *(1 mark)*

5   What do you do if you groom a dog? *(1 mark)*

6   Mrs Peach was very forgetful. Write down four things that she forgot in this passage. *(2 marks)*

7   "Sam spoke with an eye to his stomach." What does this mean? *(1 mark)*

8   Why was Mrs Peach's hair so untidy? *(1 mark)*

9   Why did Sam cross his fingers in the last paragraph? *(2 marks)*

10 Do you think Mrs Peach was a good mother? Why? *(3 marks)*

When walking do you suffer ROAD RAGE?

Walking is important

1. Walking is the "glue" binding together the transport system. It accounts for nearly a third of all journeys and 80% of journeys under a mile. Most car journeys and nearly all public transport journeys involve a walk.

2. Walking is 'the nearest activity to perfect exercise' (Sports Medicine, May 1997). Walking is good for you and cuts down on unnecessary car journeys and the associated noise and air pollution.

3. Walking is also a socially sustainable means of travel. It is free and requires no special equipment. Creating safe, pleasant areas for walking is a vital part of bringing our towns and cities back to life.

But do pedestrians get the environment they deserve?

Walking remains a major mode of travel despite the appalling condition of the walking environment.

- Britain's pavements are a disgrace. Government figures show that one in five pavements are sub-standard, and the trend is worsening. People need clean, well-maintained pavements they can walk on without fear of tripping. They also need an end to pavement parking and pavement cycling.

- Pedestrian crossings, where they exist, are often in the wrong place. Pedestrians are diverted through subways, over footbridges or made to cross a road in several stages.

- Speeding vehicles intimidate pedestrians and annually cause thousands of deaths and injuries. We need lower traffic speeds in our villages, towns and cities.

These conditions are particularly serious for people with mobility difficulties or sight problems. The walking environment needs to be designed and maintained to meet the needs of everyone, not just the young and able bodied.

The walk to school message is starting to be heard

Walking to school has been declining due to parents' fear of traffic and 'stranger danger'. This has led to increasingly unhealthy lifestyles for Britain's children. The school run forms 20% of peak morning urban congestion with the attendant increase in pollution and its damaging effect on conditions such as asthma.

The Government's recognition of the need for safe walking routes to school is a major achievement for our Walk to School campaign. The challenge now is to turn the government's words into safe, pleasant and convenient routes to all schools.

What does the Pedestrians Association do?

From its earliest days, the Pedestrians Association has been scoring successes on behalf of pedestrians. In the 1920s, our campaigns persuaded the Government to introduce the driving test, the 30mph urban speed limit and pedestrian crossings. The Pedestrians Association also helped write the very first Highway Code.

Since those early successes we have moved on to cover all aspects of pedestrian welfare.

1. We work to make walking safer, more convenient and easier, making it possible for people to leave the car at home when travelling short distances.
2. We protect and promote the rights and safety of people travelling on foot and provide information and advice to the public, other organisations and the government.

3. We work with the government, local authorities and other bodies to promote the benefits of walking as an environmentally friendly, sustainable and healthy form of transport.

Walking for all

Millions of people already walk every day. The Pedestrians Association wants to make these journeys better and encourage others to walk. If people want to walk they should be able to do so safely, and conveniently. This means better pavements, better crossings, less traffic and less pollution.

from a leaflet published by *The Pedestrians Association* (now Living Streets)

 Answer in sentences.

1 Explain how most car journeys "involve walking". *(1 mark)*

2 In what way are Britain's pavements "a disgrace"? *(1 mark)*

3 What is meant by a) pavement parking and b) pavement cycling? *(2 marks)*

4 The leaflet claims that pedestrian crossings are often in the wrong place. What would the right place be? *(1 mark)*

5 Give the meaning of the underlined words:
a) Speeding vehicles <u>intimidate</u> pedestrians... *(1 mark)*
b) ... and <u>annually</u> cause thousands of deaths and injuries. *(1 mark)*

6 What is the "school run"? *(1 mark)*

7 What two reasons are given for fewer pupils now walking to school? *(2 marks)*

8 What two kinds of pollution can cars cause? *(2 marks)*

9 Name four of the early achievements of The Pedestrians Association. *(2 marks)*

10 In what way is walking "environmentally friendly"? *(1 mark)*

UNIT 32

Population data

	A	B	C	D	E	F	G	H
	Country	Population 2004	Area (square miles)	Density population per square mile	Approx. annual birth rate (%)	Approx. annual death rate (%)	Annual growth rate (%)	Estimated population 2005
1	Australia	20,100,000	2,988,888	7	1.3	0.7	0.6	20,220,600
2	Bangladesh	141,300,000	55,598	2,541	3.0	0.9	2.1	144,267,300
3	Denmark	5,400,000	16,637	325	1.2	1.1	0.1	5,405,400
4	Egypt	73,400,000	386,660	190	2.6	0.6	2.0	74,868,000
5	France	60,000,000	212,934	282	1.3	0.9	0.4	60,240,000
6	Gambia	1,500,000	4,363	344	4.1	1.3	2.8	1,542,000
7	Germany	82,600,000	137,830	599	0.9	1.0	-0.1	82,517,400
8	Ghana	21,400,000	92,100	232	3.3	1.0	2.3	21,892,200
9	Indonesia	218,700,000	735,355	297	2.2	0.6	1.6	222,199,200
10	Ireland	4,100,000	27,135	151	1.6	0.7	0.9	4,136,900
11	Italy	57,800,000	116,320	497	1.0	1.0	0.0	57,800,000
12	Nigeria	137,300,000	356,668	385	4.2	1.3	2.9	141,281,700
13	Norway	4,600,000	125,050	37	1.2	0.9	0.3	4,613,800
14	Portugal	10,500,000	35,514	296	1.1	1.0	0.1	10,510,500
15	Russia	144,100,000	6,592,819	22	1.0	1.7	-0.7	143,091,300
16	Singapore	4,200,000	239	17,573	1.0	0.4	0.6	4,225,200
17	Turkey	71,300,000	299,158	238	2.1	0.7	1.4	72,298,200
18	United Kingdom	59,700,000	94,548	631	1.2	1.0	0.2	59,819,400
19	United States	293,600,000	3,717,796	79	1.4	0.8	0.6	295,361,600
20	Venezuela	26,200,000	352,143	74	2.4	0.5	1.9	26,697,800

In the spreadsheet above, there is information about population around the world. The information comes from the Population Reference Bureau.

What is a spreadsheet? It is a type of computer program. A spreadsheet is a table or grid that is laid out in columns, rows and

individual cells. It can be used to store numerical data and carry out calculations with it. If there are subsequent changes in the data, the effects can be easily shown.

There are three kinds of data that can be input into a spreadsheet.

1 *Text*

An example of text data is the name of the countries in column A.

2 *Numbers*

Examples of number data are those numbers in columns B, C, E, and F.

3 *Mathematical formulae*

Columns D, G and H contain numbers that have been calculated using formulae. For example, the numbers in column D have been calculated by dividing the population in column B by the area in square miles in column C. The formula for doing this has been programmed into the spreadsheet and so the spreadsheet can easily be updated.

 Answer in sentences.

1 Where has the information in this spreadsheet come from? *(1 mark)*

2 Which country has the largest population? *(2 marks)*

3 In which country is there no growth rate? *(2 marks)*

4 How many countries have a declining growth rate? *(2 marks)*

5 What information do you find in cell G12? *(2 marks)*

6 Singapore has the highest density of population. What does this mean? *(2 marks)*

7 How is the annual growth rate calculated? *(2 marks)*

8 The spreadsheet is organised by listing the countries in alphabetical order. Suggest two other ways it could be organised. *(2 marks)*

UNIT 33

The cyclone

Dorothy lived in the midst of the great Kansas prairies, with Uncle Henry, who was a farmer, and Aunt Em, who was the farmer's wife. Their house was small, for the lumber to build it had to be carried by wagon many miles. There were four walls, a floor, and a roof, which made one room; and this room contained a rusty-looking cooking stove, a cupboard for the dishes, a table, three or four chairs, and the beds. Uncle Henry and Aunt Em had a big bed in one corner and Dorothy a little bed in another corner. There was no garret at all, and no cellar – except a small hole, dug in the ground, called a cyclone cellar, where the family could go in case one of those great whirlwinds arose, mighty enough to crush any building in its path. It was reached by a trap door in the middle of the floor, from which a ladder led down into the small, dark hole.

When Dorothy stood in the doorway and looked around, she could see nothing but the great grey prairie on every side. Not a tree nor a house broke the broad sweep of flat country that reached to the edge of the sky in all directions. The sun had baked the ploughed land into a grey mass, with little cracks running through it. Even the grass was not green, for the sun had burned the tops of the long blades until they were the same grey colour to be seen everywhere. Once the house had been painted, but the sun blistered the paint and the rains washed it away, and now the house was as dull and grey as everything else.

When Aunt Em came there to live she was a young, pretty wife. The sun and wind had changed her, too. They had taken the sparkle from her eyes and left them a sober grey; they had taken the red from her cheeks and lips, and they were grey also. She was thin and gaunt, and never smiled now. When Dorothy, who was an orphan, first came to her, Aunt Em had been so startled by the child's laughter that she would scream and press her hand upon her heart whenever Dorothy's merry voice reached her ears; and she still looked at the little girl with wonder that she could find anything to laugh at.

Uncle Henry never laughed. He worked hard from morning till night and did not know what joy was. He was grey also, from his long beard to his rough boots, and he looked stern and solemn, and rarely spoke.

It was Toto that made Dorothy laugh, and saved her from growing as grey as her other surroundings. Toto was not grey; he was a little black dog, with long silky hair and small black eyes that twinkled merrily on either side of his funny, wee nose. Toto played all day long, and Dorothy played with him, and loved him dearly.

Today, however, they were not playing. Uncle Henry sat upon the doorstep and looked anxiously at the sky, which was even greyer than usual. Dorothy stood in the door with Toto in her arms, and looked at the sky too. Aunt Em was washing the dishes.

From the far north they heard a low wail of the wind, and Uncle Henry and Dorothy could see where the long grass bowed in waves before the coming storm. There now came a sharp whistling in the air from the south, and as they turned their eyes that way they saw ripples in the grass coming from that direction also.

Suddenly Uncle Henry stood up.
"There's a cyclone coming, Em," he called to his wife. "I'll go look after the stock." Then he ran towards the sheds where the cows and horses were kept.

Aunt Em dropped her work and came to the door. One glance told her of the danger close at hand.

"Quick, Dorothy!" she screamed. "Run for the cellar!"

Toto jumped out of Dorothy's arms and hid under the bed, and the girl started to get him. Aunt Em, badly frightened, threw open the trap door in the floor and climbed down the ladder into the small, dark hole. Dorothy caught Toto at last, and started to follow her aunt. When she was halfway across the room there came a great shriek from the wind, and the house shook so hard that she lost her footing and sat down suddenly upon the floor.

A strange thing then happened.

The house whirled around two or three times and rose slowly through the air. Dorothy felt as if she were going up in a balloon.

The north and south winds met where the house stood, and made it the exact centre of the cyclone. In the middle of a cyclone the air is generally still, but the great pressure of the wind on every side of the house raised it up higher and higher, until it was at the very top of the cyclone; and there it remained and was carried miles and miles away as easily as you could carry a feather.

It was very dark, and the wind howled horribly around her, but Dorothy found she was riding quite easily. After the first few whirls around, and one other time when the house tipped badly, she felt as if she were being rocked gently, like a baby in a cradle.

L. Frank Baum from
The Wonderful Wizard of Oz (Puffin)

Answer in sentences.

1   "There was no garret at all". What is another word for "garret"?
    (1 mark)

2   What is the reason given in the passage to explain why the house was so
    small? *(1 mark)*

3   What other evidence is there that Uncle Henry and Aunt Em are poor?
    (1 mark)

4   Describe the cyclone cellar and explain why it had been built. *(2 marks)*

5   What word in the first paragraph means "cyclones"? *(1 mark)*

6   Aunt Em is "thin and gaunt". Explain the difference in meaning
    between these two adjectives. *(1 mark)*

7   In one stage adaptation of the novel, Toto is a pet mouse. What is he in
    the novel here? *(1 mark)*

8   What do Aunt Em's lips, Uncle Henry's beard, the ploughed earth and
    the grass of the prairie have in common? *(1 mark)*

9   How different would Dorothy's life be without Toto? *(1 mark)*

10 The wind wails and whistles as it approaches. What sound does it make
    when it reaches the house? *(1 mark)*

11 How can Aunt Em tell with "one glance" that the cyclone is coming?
    (1 mark)

12 Uncle Henry runs to look after "the stock". What does this mean?
    (1 mark)

13 When the house whirled up in the air, Dorothy felt "as if she were going
    up in a balloon" and so she didn't feel at all frightened. Find two more
    comparisons in the next two paragraphs that describe how gently the
    house was carried along. *(2 marks)*

Dictionary of composers

Bach, Johann Sebastian (1685–1750), German composer

Probably one of the greatest composers of all time, J.S. Bach is famous for his cantatas and choral works, (including the "St. Matthew Passion") and for his many chamber and orchestral pieces (including the six "Brandenburg Concertos"). All his family were musical; there were more than sixty musical Bachs by the time the family died out in the 1800s. Bach was married twice and had twenty children, three of whom became famous musicians and composers.

Beethoven, Ludwig van (1770–1827), German composer

Beethoven became severely deaf by the age of 32. Despite his initial despair, he found the inner strength to compose powerful works which were to establish him as a giant among composers. His nine magnificent symphonies, his opera "Fidelio", 48 sonatas, 17 string quartets, 10 overtures and dozens of other pieces all bear witness to his genius. Some of his finest works, e.g. the "Ninth Symphony", were written in the last years of his life. He could not hear them in performance. He could not even hear the applause.

Berlioz, Hector (1803–1869), French composer

Berlioz, initially training as a doctor, gave up his medical studies (much to his father's annoyance) to study music at the Paris Conservatoire, making a living subsequently as a music critic and conductor. In 1830, he composed his "Symphonie Fantastique", still his most popular work. He loved the plays of Shakespeare, and based a number of his symphonies on them, such as "Roméo et Juliette".

Brahms, Johannes (1833–1897), German composer

Brahms was taught the piano at a young age by his father, a double-bass player. As a boy he helped to support the family by playing in inns and cafés. He began composing and was encouraged to continue by the composer, Robert Schumann. Fame came in 1868 with the performance of "The German Requiem". All of his finest work was written after this, including four symphonies, concertos, chamber music and nearly 200 songs. He composed in all musical forms except opera.

Britten, Benjamin (1913–1976), English composer

Britten began composing music at the age of five, and his "Simple Symphony" is made up of tunes that he wrote as a child. He is famous for his orchestral and choral music, including the much-loved "War Requiem" and for his operas which include "Peter Grimes", "Billy Budd", "Turn of the Screw" and "Death in Venice". "Let's Make an Opera" was composed for children and is written in such a way that children can join in. His "Young Person's Guide to the Orchestra", as its name suggests, was also written for children and introduces each of the orchestral instruments in turn.

Write out the sentences that are true. *(2 marks for finding each correct statement plus 1 mark for careful writing)*

1   If George Bizet were included here, he would follow Hector Berlioz.

2   The "German Requiem" was composed by Johannes Brahms.

3   There were more than sixty musical Beethovens by the time the family died out in the 1800s.

4   Beethoven and Berlioz were both alive in 1826.

5   Beethoven wrote his "Ninth Symphony" when he was very young.

6   Brahms' family were quite poor.

7   Bach had twenty children.

8   "Severely" deaf means "slightly" deaf.

9   Benjamin Britten began composing when he was five years old.

10   As well as being a composer, Hector Berlioz was a qualified doctor.

11   Ludwig van Beethoven had to stop composing when he became deaf.

12   "Symphonie Fantastique" was written before Berlioz was 30 years old.

U N I T
35

Gingernuts

Make these delicious gingernut biscuits and you'll never want to buy shop ones again. This recipe makes 16 biscuits.

You will need:
110g self-raising flour
1 slightly rounded teaspoon ground ginger
1 teaspoon bicarbonate of soda
40g sugar
50g butter or margarine
2 tablespoons golden syrup

Preheat the oven to Gas Mark 5, 190° C, 375° F
Lightly grease two shallow baking trays about 30cm by 25cm, or use one baking tray and cook in two batches.

1 Sieve the flour, ginger, and bicarbonate of soda into a large bowl. Mix well.
2 Add the butter or margarine cut into small pieces, and rub into the mixture with your fingertips until the mixture looks just like breadcrumbs.
3 Add the sugar and mix well.
4 Add the golden syrup, and mix first with a spoon and then with your fingers until you can form the mixture into a ball of soft dough.
5 Turn the dough on to a clean work surface, and make into a long sausage. Cut the sausage into 16 equal pieces. Roll each piece into a ball in the palms of your hands.

6 Arrange the balls of dough, eight to each baking tray, well apart, because they spread flat as they are cooking. Flatten each one slightly with the back of a metal spoon.

7 Cook just above the centre of the oven for 10–15 minutes. Take care not to burn yourself on the hot interior of the oven. You may like to ask an adult to help you.

8 When they are cooked, leave the biscuits to cool on the baking tray. They will become crisp as they cool. Then transfer to a wire rack to cool completely. Store in an airtight tin.

Answer in sentences.

1   Which word here means "items baked together"? *(2 marks)*

2   What does "preheat" mean? *(2 marks)*

3   Why do you think that you are advised to make the dough into a long sausage before dividing it into 16 pieces? *(2 marks)*

4   How can you tell that the biscuits are going to be soft when they are taken out of the oven? *(2 marks)*

5   Why is it important "to mix well" at various stages? *(3 marks)*

6   What would happen to the biscuits in the oven if you placed them too close together? *(2 marks)*

7   Explain why the cooked biscuits cannot be transferred immediately to a wire rack. *(2 marks)*

UNIT 36 Comparison of poetic forms

Kennings Cat (kenning)

Tail-flicker
Fur-licker
Tree-scratcher
Mouse-catcher
Basket-sleeper
Night-creeper
Eye-blinker
Milk-drinker
Lap-sitter
Ball-hitter
Fish-eater
Fire-heater
String-muddler
Kitten-cuddler
Angry-hisser
Wet-kisser
Wall-prowler
Moon-howler
Cream-lapper
Claw-tapper
Cat-flapper

Sandy Brownjohn from *Both Sides of the Catflap* (Hodder Children's books)

LARK
(thin poem)

spi
inn
ng
at
the
pe
ak
of
an
inv
isi
ble
je
t o
f w
ate
r,
you
bu
rn
a b
lac
k s
tar
at
th
e h
ear
t o
f t
he
blu
e a
ppl
e w
e c
all
sk
y,
LARK.

George Macbeth from *Pen Rhythms*
ed. Chris Webster (Stanley Thornes)

Revolver II

Alan Riddell from *Pen Rhythms*
ed. Chris Webster (Stanley Thornes)

Snake (shape poem)

Snake glides
   through grass
     over
       pebbles
        forked tongue
    working
  never
speaking
  but its
    body
      whispers
      listen

Keith Bosley from *O Frabjous Day!*
selected by Sandy Brownjohn (Ginn)

The Fastest Train in the World
Tokyo to Kyoto (haiku)

tokyotokyoto
kyotokyotokyotokyo
tokyotokyoto

Keith Bosley from *O Frabjous Day!* selected by Sandy Brownjohn (Ginn)

 Answer in sentences.

1   Sandy Brownjohn calls her cat a lot of lovely names in "Kennings Cat"! Which two kennings refer to the sounds her cat can make? *(1 mark)*

2   Why do the last three kennings make a very good ending to the poem? *(2 marks)*

3   Write down two adjectives that would describe how Sandy Brownjohn feels about her cat. *(2 marks)*

4   "You can enjoy 'The Fastest Train in the World' just by looking at the way it is set out." Give the reasons why you agree or disagree with this statement. *(2 marks)*

5   As you look at "Revolver II", which two words can you see clearly? *(1 mark)*

6   Write out "Lark" as a sentence. *(1 mark)*

7   Why is the lark described as a "black star"? *(1 mark)*

8   What does "Lark" gain by being set out as a thin poem? *(1 mark)*

9   What is it about the snake he describes that fascinates Keith Bosley? *(2 marks)*

10 Which of these poems did you enjoy the most? Try to explain the reasons for your choice. *(2 marks)*